Ginny and Her Horses

Ginny and Her Horses

Virginia Leng with Genevieve Murphy

Stanley Paul

London   Melbourne   Auckland   Johannesburg

Stanley Paul & Co. Ltd

An imprint of Century Hutchinson Ltd

Brookmount House, 62–65 Chandos Place
Covent Garden, London WC2N 4NW

Century Hutchinson Australia (Pty) Ltd
PO Box 496, 16–22 Church Street,
Hawthorn, Melbourne, Victoria 3122

Century Hutchinson New Zealand Limited
191 Archers Road, PO Box 40–086,
Glenfield, Auckland 10

Century Hutchinson South Africa (Pty) Ltd
PO Box 337, Bergvlei 2012, South Africa

Set in Bembo

Printed and bound in Great Britain by
Butler & Tanner Ltd,
Frome and London

British Library Cataloguing in Publication Data

Leng, Virginia
    Ginny and her horses.
    1. Leng, Virginia 2. Show jumpers (Persons)
    —Great Britain—Biography
    I. Title II. Murphy, Genevieve
    798.2′4′0924   SF 295.5

ISBN   0 09 172652 2

ACKNOWLEDGEMENTS

Thanks are due to Kit Houghton for supplying the majority of the photographs that appear in this book. Other photographs are by (black and white) Peter Ayres, Hugo Czerny, Martin Dalby, Findlay Davidson, Peter Doresa, Mike Freeman, Elizabeth Furth, Clive Hiles, Jim Meads, Trevor Meeks, Steve Yarnell; (colour) Equestrian Services Thorney, Mike Freeman, Stuart Newsham, Steve Yarnell.

CONTENTS

CHAPTER ONE

The Stars of Ivyleaze

Someone once asked my husband, Hamish, 'What is it like to be married to a star?'

'I have absolutely no idea,' he replied. 'You'd better ask Ginny.'

To my mind, if Big Ham will forgive me saying so, the real stars are the horses. It is their four legs, their immense courage and willingness to please, that have carried me to the successes I have had the great good fortune to enjoy. Horses are like people, as my mother and Dorothy Willis would tell you – and as the girls who put in so much hard work in the stables would confirm. They are all individuals with their own special quirks, their likes and dislikes.

We, the human minders, are constantly striving to get the delicate balance between kindness and discipline right so that the horses can produce the best performance of which they are capable. We have a mixed bunch to work with in the stables and fields around Ivyleaze, my mother's house at Acton Turville which is just a mile from Badminton.

Priceless, who used to be our Sergeant Major, is temporarily absent. He left to go hunting with my great friend, Louise Bates, after he had retired at the end of 1986. Night Cap is very much the officer and gentleman – good-looking, charming and always anxious to please. Murphy Himself is more the John McEnroe type; he is butch, tough and very talented, with a bit of a temper and a pronounced argumentative streak.

Master Craftsman, the most mature of the younger horses that I ride, would make head boy in a rather smart prep school. Being thoroughbred, he has a well-to-do, clean-cut look about him and is very confident,

Big Ham and little Gin

7

without being cocky. He is good-looking, easy-going and very fast; he would definitely shine on the school's sports day. But, since he does not stand any nonsense from other horses, the boys would have to watch their step.

Ballyhack would be a menace, the sort of boy any self-respecting teacher would loathe to have in his class. He would wear his tie crooked and spend most of his time firing catapults; he would be cocky and unruly, thinking of no one but himself. Money Broker who was with us for about six months before being sold, would be the exact opposite. He is the shy introvert, anxious to please everyone but a bit afraid to speak up. If they were at a party, Money Broker would stand in a corner wondering whether he dared talk to anyone, while Ballyhack would be in the noisiest group making a complete fool of himself. If Ballyhack and Murphy were there together, they would probably have a punch-up.

Louise Bates's Sapperhill came to us in the summer of 1987, after Money Broker had left, so I still had five partners to ride. We also had four horses being ridden by Mandy Hosp, who joined us the previous year, and one eventing with Elaine Pickworth, who used to look after Priceless. There were also two four-year-old babies and a grand old man of twenty-one called Dubonnet, who was the first horse I rode in a three-day event.

Normally a couple of familiar faces disappear each year. We need to sell two of the horses we have been schooling in order to make ends meet, but these are usually replaced by youngsters. My mother can never resist buying a horse that looks as though it will make a top eventer, always assuming that the price is right. She has made some marvellous purchases over the years, but there have also been many fruitless journeys to see horses that were not, to put it kindly, quite the type she was looking for!

I am, of course, hugely indebted to my wonderful sponsors at Citibank Savings (formerly British National Life Assurance), where Paul Cohen is managing director and Val Gates, a former Olympic athlete herself, is the public relations officer who keeps in close contact with the Ivyleaze team. I would never have been able to keep going without their support which began with an initial three-year contract in 1981. This was renewed in 1984 and again, to my great relief and delight, in 1987. I am also enormously grateful to Spillers for the help they give us in feeding our hungry horses.

Every member of the human team at Ivyleaze has a part to play. I ride the horses, as does Mandy who also looks after some of them. My mother is in charge of schooling and breaking the youngsters; she is responsible for the early fittening work with horses we are preparing for a three-day event and she is in charge of feeding both humans and horses. Dorothy (usually known as Dot) lunges the horses, looks after the equipment, gives

Team truck driver, Heather Holgate, with her urchin daughter

lessons to the girls and keeps an eagle eye on my flat work in between my sessions with Pat Manning. Nicky and Anna look after the remaining horses.

Elaine, who used to take care of Priceless, is now in charge of the paperwork. This used to be the province of our former secretary Maita who was closely involved with us for about 6 years, from the time I rode in my first Senior European Championships. Maita moved to Hong Kong

Below: *Badminton, 1985. Night Cap on his way to third place*

Right: *Murphy is bold and stylish at Stowell Park, 1987*

when her husband landed a super job there as an airline pilot for Cathay Pacific. Sue (McMahon) comes to us once a week and helps to school some of our younger horses on the flat. She has also taken one of them, Benevolent, home with her to school and ride in dressage competitions.

Other frequent visitors include our brilliant vet (Don Attenburrow), our farrier (Robert Hall) who always puts on the go-faster-jump-higher-do-better shoes before a three-day event, and Pat Manning who has been my dressage trainer for 16 years. We also think of the village of Acton Turville as part of our team – especially our local policeman, P C Earl and his wife, the Beasleys who run the village stores, and Howard at the local garage whom we sometimes call out at five o'clock in the morning because the lorry has refused to start.

Needless to say, the most important visitor of all is my husband. To answer that initial question, it feels wonderful being married to a star, especially one who gives me so much support and encouragement. For-

Left: *Ben Hovis knows that this is his own pad*

Below: *At home in the cottage, where there is endless paperwork to be done*

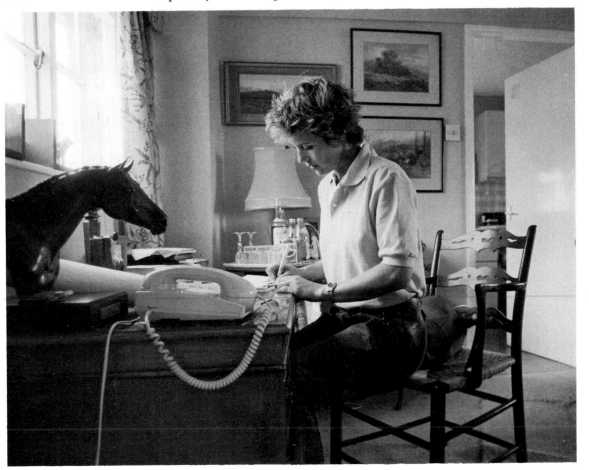

tunately, Hamish has never wanted to have a wife who stays at home and looks after the nest the whole time. Though I have acquired a passion for cooking, it would not be true to say that my husband has regarded every one of my experiments in the kitchen as an unqualified success!

Hamish is based in London and he works harder than anyone I know. He is up before 6 a.m. each morning and in his office by about 6.30 to start his day's work as financial consultant and partner in J. L. Associates. He is rarely home before 9 p.m. and, when he goes out for dinner, he is back much later – but he still gets up at the same ungodly hour the following morning. I am constantly amazed by his stamina.

I am based at Ivyleaze, in a cottage behind the house, where my own timetable is far less severe. Hamish joins me most weekends (leaving between 4.30 and 5.30 a.m. to get to work on the Monday morning) and I join him in London every ten days or so. It means that we are never together as much as we would wish. I regard it as a wonderful treat when we manage to get away on holiday – or for a long weekend like the one we had at Easter, 1987, with our friends in Cornwall. It was good to have a break from horse talk; to play golf, tennis and Trivial Pursuit, with all those questions which I could never answer.

The cottage at Ivyleaze is tiny, which normally limits the number of people we invite to a dinner party. We have a round table in the kitchen, where four people can sit in reasonable comfort and six at a pinch. We

Jack of all trades, Howard Richardson (garage owner and horsebox builder) discussing alterations for our lorry

did fit ten people in there one evening, which was an interesting experience if you enjoy being packed like sardines!

We are hoping to have an extra room built on to the cottage so that we have a little more space and Hamish can work in peace at weekends, away from the kitchen where there are always people coming and going. When he has finished his financial work, Hamish loves gardening and he often gives my mother a hand outside, which is much appreciated.

Marriage has given me some indoor interests. Apart from my new found love of cooking, I have become increasingly involved in interior decorating – if that is not too grand a way of describing my efforts with the flat in London. They are frequently frustrated by my forgetfulness. I can go into Bath or Bristol with measurements for new curtains, only to realize that I can't remember the colour of the walls.

Hamish obviously has many friends in London and I love meeting them for dinner or at the theatre – or better still, both. You can live so much in a cocoon in the horse world that it would be easy to lose your outside interests, which I'm sure is a mistake.

We naturally spend a fair amount of our time talking horses at Ivyleaze. When we have a problem or are trying to decide on the right event for a particular horse, there may be a two-hour discussion between my mother, Dot and myself. Sometimes Hamish joins in. He has been watching me often enough to be able to recognize my style and there are times

The indispensible village shop. Left to right: Anne and George Beasley with Jean Earl (our policeman's wife) and one of their regular customers from Ivyleaze

when he can pinpoint something that my mother and Dot, who see me riding every day, may have failed to notice.

Big Ham says that he finds it easy to recognize me on a cross-country course. Apparently I have the same forward seat when I am watching television!

Left to right: Lucinda Green, myself, Mike Tucker, Lorna Clarke and Tiny Clapham, pre Frauenfeld, 1983

CHAPTER TWO

Officer and Gentleman

Night Cap is such a perfect gentleman at home that not one of us has been able to come up with a single story about him that might raise a chuckle. Unlike some of our naughtier horses, he has been anxious to please from the day my mother bought him as a three-year-old. As Dot says: 'Night Cap is a gentle person, who would never think ill of anybody; he's so good that you would find it hard not to love him.'

He is Nicky Ide-Smith's favourite horse at Ivyleaze, partly because she has looked after him since she joined us in September 1984. 'He has such a nice temperament, though he can be very ticklish to groom when his muscles are fit and tight,' she says. 'Then his ears go back and his tail starts swishing, but he retaliates by attacking the beam in his stable rather than having a go at me. If he catches me by mistake, he gets himself in a real twitter and looks at me as much as to say, "Sorry mate, it was the wrong beam!".'

We were living in Devon when we first spotted Night Cap in a field down the road. He was a two-year-old, owned by John Chapel who had bought him as a yearling from his breeder, Sir Edward Mallet. My mother, who has never tired of looking at horses that might be for sale, examined the youngster many times with her eagle eye. 'If you feel like selling the horse, do let us know when you've backed him,' she said to John.

So one day John arrived at our place riding Night Cap, who was going so sweetly that we assumed he had been backed many months before.

'What about jumping?' we asked, pointing to a very nasty ditch in our field.

'No problem,' said John, proving this was true by jumping the ditch with amazing ease on the handsome young horse, who is by Diana Scott's stallion Ben Faerie.

It was afterwards, during a casual conversation, that we discovered he had been backed for the first time that morning. Thanks to his kind and generous nature, the idea of refusing to jump that nasty ditch had not so much as crossed his mind.

In some ways Night Cap is too tractable for his own good. He has always listened to his rider, anxious to do whatever I might have been asking him even when my judgement was at fault. Had he been a little more aggressive, he might have ignored my signals on those occasions and used his own talent more effectively. He has won many competitions, but I feel that I let him down on some important occasions when I was desperately trying to learn how to ride him.

He had one refusal at his first Badminton in 1984, when I under-rode him, and another in the European Championships the same year at Frauenfeld in Switzerland, which was a more blatant example of rider's error. The single stop in Switzerland came at the end of the course, on a day of exhausting heat with the temperature high in the eighties. I was

Going, going . . .

last to go for the British team and anxious to prove worthy of such a responsible place. Lucinda Green, who had already jumped a fantastic clear round on Regal Realm, told me how the course was riding – with particular emphasis on the problems that had occurred at fence 28, a row of barrels with two strides on the landing side before fairly deep water. I needed to ride into it slowly, on a short bouncy stride; all those who had gone in fast had taken a ducking.

Foolishly, I rode in too slowly and we lost all our forward impulsion; Night Cap stopped in front of the barrels for an expensive 20 penalties that were entirely my fault. I reached an all-time low in self-destructive remorse afterwards, as I agonized over my idiotic mistake on video at home and wondered whether I should give up the sport. I do not pretend to understand the mysterious workings of the Good Lord, but I felt He had answered my prayers and put an end to the fretful soul-sourching when Priceless and I won Burghley a few weeks after Frauenfeld.

Night Cap and Priceless (otherwise known as N and P) are both the same age. But they are totally different in all other respects; it took me far longer to learn how to ride the gentle and responsive N than the quick-witted and bossy P. I had still not got it together when I over-rode Night Cap to the fence out of the lake at Badminton the following year and fell there. After that fall I found a particularly relevant prayer, which Dot had pinned on my kitchen notice board. 'Oh Lord, grant me the serenity to accept those things I cannot change, the courage to change the things I can and the wisdom to know the difference.' I have said these words to myself on many occasions and they have helped me through the general ups and downs of life, which are by no means confined to sport.

Night Cap's one and only irritating trait was his tendency to become overwrought in the dressage phase of a big three-day event, where he reacted to the crowds – and, more especially, to the sound of clapping. He is capable of doing a superlative test, but he needed to be calm and relaxed if he were to use his natural talent to the full.

We had tried various ploys during the summer months after the fall at Badminton – four days at the Bath and West Show, a visit to the local football match, clapping from a rent-a-crowd at home, brass-band music in his stable. He was still tense when I rode him at Burghley in the autumn but, even though I knew he could have done a better dressage test, he succeeded in following in P's footsteps by winning the three-day event which was sponsored, for the second year, by Remy Martin.

A new and more effective ploy was tried before the dressage phase of the 1985 Whitbread Championships at Badminton, when we gave N a couple of hours to soak up the atmosphere and unwind before his test. We reduced the time for his flat work (he doesn't need to be worked in

gone! Night Cap at Badminton, 1984

for long); he was then led around and allowed to pick at grass in the collecting ring while he listened to the clapping and eventually became bored by it.

Having delighted me with a good test, he went on to be clear in the cross-country and show jumping to finish third at Badminton that year; but he was still in the shadow of his stablemate, Priceless, who won. P was in quarantine for the World Championships when I took N to the 1986 Badminton, where I was again thrilled with his dressage – but less so with my riding at the fences through the lake, where he had a single run-out. He had been first to tackle the cross-country course, made sodden after torrential rain on the two dressage days, and we finished in fourth place behind Ian Stark, who won on Sir Wattie.

Night Cap did not see as much as usual of his rider during the months that followed. He was left in the capable hands of Nicky while my mother, Dot and I were in Australia with Priceless for the World Championships, and in France the following month with Murphy for the three-day event at Le Touquet. N was being aimed for the Polish event at Bialy Bor when I took him, with Priceless and Murphy, to the British National Championships at Gatcombe. Foolishly, I agreed to take part in the Land-Rover race on the same day that I was riding all three horses across country and it was typical that Night Cap should be the one to suffer from my silly attempt to do too much.

Because the Land-Rover race was running late I had only ten minutes to get on Night Cap and prepare to set off across country; I was in a flutter and not mentally ready for the job in hand. Even Hamish said that he had never seen my concentration lapse so badly. N was wondering what on earth was going on, while I was trying to unscramble my wits; neither of us really got going to attack the fences. Then I failed to see a stride at a double of corners, so N had to put in a short one. He tried to take off and finished with his front legs on the fence; I had to turn him back (for an expensive 20 penalties) and jump the slow route.

The Gatcombe hiccup left me worrying about our forthcoming three-day event in Poland, until we had a morale-boosting outing in the Scottish Championships at Thirlestane Castle, where N jumped a lovely clear round. I rode Murphy at Burghley before making an easy trip by air to Poland, with the other British riders, while my mother (the amazing Yorkie Bar Kid) was co-driver of the horsebox, in which Dot and Nicky were passengers, on that very long road journey from the Hook of Holland.

'I love driving the Volvo,' says my mother, referring to the horsebox, 'so I didn't set out in fear and trepidation of a long journey; I was looking forward to the trip.'

Night Cap on his way to winning Burghley, 1984

They sailed to the Hook of Holland and then set off in a small convoy – our lorry and another belonging to John and Jane Thelwall, two Range Rovers and the Isuzu, which (along with the smart red Porsche my mother and I drive) had been kindly provided for us by the London firm, Charles Follett Ltd. Chef d'équipe Lord Patrick Beresford and team vet Peter Scott-Dunn drove the Range Rovers; the team farrier, Keith Watson, was behind the wheel of the Isuzu.

My mother was sharing the driving with Andrew Wardle, who runs the shipping agency that we frequently use. He sat in the front passenger seat as they left the Hook, with the map spread out in front of him, saying: 'Don't worry, Heather, it's motorway all the way.' This comforting – but, alas, inaccurate – information was apparently repeated at frequent intervals as my mother drove the lorry down a seemingly endless succession of narrow roads. Occasionally they did find themselves on a stretch of Dutch motorway, but it then petered out after about five miles.

They lunched in Germany, where they mucked out the lorries and fed the local roses, before driving on to Wolfenbuttle near the East German border, to spend a night as guests of the 9th/12th Lancers who were exceptionally kind to them all. They had time to explore this beautiful old town on their return journey, when the other lorry broke down, but it was full steam ahead to Poland on the outward trip with an early morning start for the border.

'It felt quite eerie,' says my mother, as she recalls driving through the checkpoint while Andrew dealt with the paperwork. 'There was a platform level with the window of the lorry, with people walking up and down, peering into the vehicle and talking to each other in rapid German. I couldn't understand a single word.'

Andrew drove across East Germany to the Polish border, where, if anything, they were even stricter. Every single penny they had on them had to be accounted for, both on the outward and return journeys. 'We were all feeling slightly tense,' says my mother, 'and when someone from our group tapped on the door, poor Dorothy nearly went through the roof of the lorry!'

They stopped at a stud in Poland for two nights, glad to have a break after two full days of driving and knowing that there was one more to come. Though the Polish roads had scarcely any traffic, driving was made hazardous by the people who kept stepping out from woods straight onto the road, hoping to sell the mushrooms they had gathered in the forest.

My mother felt that she would never again complain about anything, after seeing what life was like for the wonderful Polish people under Communist rule. Fortunately, no one at the border crossings had bothered about the vast quantities of food crammed into all five vehicles on the

British convoy. Most of it was given away, which made us all feel slightly less guilty when we ate the excellent food that was prepared especially for the visitors.

One large bag of goodies was given to a little old lady who was sitting on a bench outside the tiny church which we quite often visited during our stay. 'She was so overcome that she wouldn't take it at first,' says my mother, who had heaped things into the bag for her. 'Then she had a word with the priest, who must have told her that it would be alright to accept it. I've never seen a little old lady move so fast once she had that bag in her hand.'

As usual, my mother and Dot lived in the lorry, while I stayed in one of the comfortable holiday chalets that were provided for the riders. The Polish people had worked incredibly hard to make this event a great success and there was only one aspect of Bialy Bor that did not really suit my book. The dressage arena happened to be in the middle of the wood, making it impossible for us to implement our latest ploy with Night Cap.

Night Cap at Bialy Bor, 1986. No efforts had been spared in creating this beautiful dressage arena

There was nowhere within sight of the arena where he could stand and graze, soaking up the atmosphere. But, though we felt it might be a problem for N, we had to agree that the setting was beautiful. A space had been cleared and levelled in the woods; permanent grandstands had been built and there were three little pine houses for the judges. It looked like a set for Hansel and Gretel.

I was the first to face the judges in their wooden houses. Having agreed to lead the way for the team (followed by Madeleine Gurdon, Rachel Hunt and Ian Stark) I found that I would be first to go in the entire competition. People were still moving into the grandstands when I did my test in the early morning sunshine, aware that Night Cap was not as relaxed as he had been at Badminton. But he was still in the lead when the two days of dressage were completed.

On cross-country day, N gave me the best ride over a steeplechase course that I have ever had on any horse; he met every fence perfectly and gave me a tremendous lift. I was brought down to earth rather smartly when I pulled up for Nicky to check his shoes. 'Stop,' she said, in a loud and urgent voice, 'there's blood pouring from his leg.'

I looked down to see blood pumping through the protective bandage on his near hind. We had no extra bandage to put on; it had never been on our list of items to be taken to the steeplechase – although it has obviously been added since. Aware that we were in trouble, the American farrier and Sharon Schneidmann, wife of one of the competitors, ran over to see if they could help – showing, through their generosity, the wonderful sportsmanship that makes three-day eventing so special. They, thank God, did have a bandage. We wound it round Night Cap's leg, checked that he was sound and I carried on, while Nicky hurried to the box to let our team vet, Peter Scott-Dunn, know what had happened.

Throughout the section of roads and tracks that followed the steeple-chase, I was concerned that the leg might still be bleeding and was constantly leaning down to look at it. All was well until we reached the box and Peter removed the bandage; blood then started pumping out of his leg again, although there was so sign of a wound. It stopped when another bandage was applied, leaving us with exactly four minutes to decide whether or not I should go across country.

'I'll start and see how he feels,' I said. 'If in any doubt, I'll pull up.'

My fears subsided after we had cleared the first five obstacles on a big and beautifully built cross-country course, with many upright fences that took some jumping. Night Cap, who had seemed happy enough as he moved along with ears pricked on the roads and tracks, was still in fine form. He gave me a cracking ride on the rather dead sandy going and finished just one second over the optimum time, which was a great thrill.

It was also nice to report that a couple of short cuts, which Madeleine Gurdon and I had discovered, really did work.

N's leg had a tiny puncture, probably caused by a sharp needle on the chopped Christmas trees used for building the steeplechase fences. It produced a dramatic amount of blood because it happened to pierce a vein, but was otherwise insignificant. Having retained our lead in the individual and team placings, I was confident that N would pass the vets the following day and went off to enjoy myself at a buffet supper and party, laid on by our hospitable Polish hosts.

When we danced that evening, one of the Russian contingent began to get rather amorous. Since Hamish had not been able to get to Poland, Rodney Powell (competing there as an individual) pretended to be my irate husband – and he earned my grateful thanks by rescuing me.

Night Cap had passed the vetting, as had our other team horses, when we all walked the show-jumping course the next day. The fences were rather spindly and airy, with very little filling that might have given them

It is not often that we have to jump on and off a house!

a more substantial look. Horses always jump much better over fences of substance and we were not surprised that they produced only four clear rounds. David O'Connor of the United States had one of them on Border Raider and he was my nearest rival when I went in, last to jump in the usual reverse order of merit, knowing that I could afford only one mistake. Though N jumped the first half of the course well, I was aware that slowly but surely he was starting to flatten; the fences were too flimsy in appearance to hold his respect. He had a rail down in the treble and I thought a later one had fallen as well to leave us in second place, though with the team still well in front.

An individual win for the United States would not have seemed inappropriate considering that I was only able to continue after the steeplechase because of help from the Americans. I was patting Night Cap and thinking: Never mind – eh (a phrase learnt from Dot, who used it so often that we bought her a T-shirt with the inscription on it) when everyone started to congratulate me.

'Didn't we have two down?' I asked in bewilderment.

'No, you only had one.'

I hope that I had not been looking miserable before I heard those words, but they certainly made me smile more brightly! It had been a fantastic year already, with Priceless winning the World Championship and Murphy scoring at Le Touquet and Burghley. It was made perfect by this success on the gentle Night Cap, whom I had let down on too many important occasions in the past.

I flew back to England and heard later that the return journey had some distressing moments for those who went by road. As they drove towards the Polish border they apparently saw trucks, crammed with horses, heading for East Germany where they were to be slaughtered. At one stage, Patrick Beresford had to drive ahead to get some papers stamped and, when he met up with the rest of the party, he told my mother he was very pleased that she had not been with him. He had gone to an abattoir when getting the papers sorted out and the sights there had been even more distressing.

Before they were allowed to cross from East to West Germany, large and incredibly efficient dogs searched the vehicles for hidden humans. My mother and Nicky watched another lorry, which was covered by a tarpaulin, being searched by a German Shepherd Dog who knew exactly what he was supposed to do. A ladder was placed against the vehicle; the dog ran straight up it and then wormed his way under the tarpaulin. He would certainly have found any person who had been unwise enough to hide there.

Night Cap, who behaved as impeccably as always on the long journey

Bialy Bor, 1986. Night Cap didn't know I had a Polish fan!

home, went out to grass with Murphy that winter while Priceless (his usual companion) began a new life after being retired to the hunting field. We wondered whether the argumentative Irishman would make life hell for the well-behaved gentleman but, if anything, it was Night Cap who ruled the roost. He resisted Murphy's fairly mild attempts to start an argument and won his respect.

They both started fittening work in January 1987, in preparation for Badminton. I was hoping that Murphy would finish in the top ten, but would dearly have loved Night Cap to win; he was fourteen years old, had spent too many years in the shadow of his stable-mates and I knew it might be his last chance.

N encouraged these cherished hopes by winning the advanced classes at Weston Park and Brigstock one-day events. His dressage was brilliant, better than it had ever been, and we were confident that we could get him to unwind sufficiently before his test at Badminton. But it was not to be.

I was hacking Murphy along the road to Badminton, with Nicky on Night Cap, when we met my mother returning in the lorry that carried all our equipment. The car parks were waterlogged and the 1987 Badminton Three-Day event had been cancelled just two days before it was due to start. Nicky and I rode on through Badminton village in the pouring rain and I popped into the Horse Trials office to say how sorry I was about the cancellation to Colonel Frank Weldon (director and course designer of the event) and the girls who work there.

They are always amazingly thorough; nothing at Badminton is either overlooked or left to chance and it will be a sad day for eventing when Frank Weldon finally retires. His cross-country courses are consistently brilliant; I don't believe there is anyone else capable of designing the same type of bold and demanding fences, which have made Badminton such a unique challenge.

I had been looking forward to jumping them in 1987 and I am sure the same is true of the horses. Both Night Cap and Murphy must have felt the tension building up towards the big event and, having watched the lorry being loaded, they were really sharp as we hacked them down the road towards the sodden park. I knew it would be grossly unfair to take them as far as the stables, where there would still be plenty of people milling around to add to their sense of expectancy, so we turned them back home. I felt that the horses were cheesed off – and I know that I was. Feeling terribly disappointed, I took myself off to Bath and consoled myself by spending far more than I should have done by buying some new clothes.

CHAPTER THREE

An Argumentative Irish Boy

If you were to pick the right moment to visit Murphy Himself in his stable, you could easily jump to a totally wrong conclusion and think that butter would never melt in his mouth. The big grey, who has a few chestnut hairs from his mother's side of the family, loves to be loved. I can hold his head in my arms and stroke his face, knowing that he laps it up. But patting him from the saddle is quite another matter.

Murphy is highly intelligent, with a mind of his own that is by no means always in accord with the ideas of his rider. He can be a bully and a con man; he can shake with excitement at the prospect of galloping and puff at the sight of a steep hill if he thinks he might have to go up it. I think he is wonderful, though I have to admit that he is far from perfect.

My first sight of Murphy's intelligent grey head was on a bleak November day in 1982, which was made bleaker for me because Priceless was desperately ill. I was reluctantly on my way to a cocktail party being given by my sponsors, and had decided to stop off and look at this Irish-bred youngster who had been advertised for sale in *Horse and Hound*.

I loved his head immediately and was thrilled when I saw him trotting because of his marvellous action. He then attempted to run out three times at some cross poles and poor Ann Verden-Jones, who had bought him earlier that year, was painfully embarrassed. Having shown me that he had a mind of his own, he went on to jump some quite big fences and I decided to take the plunge.

'I'll have him subject to the vet's examination,' I said, my heart thump-

ing at the realization that this was the first horse I had ever bought on my own. I phoned home, with the feeling that I had been terribly rash, to tell my mother – and it was probably just as well that surprise made her speechless! It was equally fortunate that both she and Dot gave their approval to the grey newcomer when he arrived at our yard.

Ann Verden-Jones, who has followed Murphy's career with great interest, tells me that he was a monster to break. 'He bucked everyone off – right, left and centre. We then decided to put the saddle on, tie some leather boots to it and turn him loose in the outdoor school. He went completely bananas and eventually jumped out, falling in a heap on the far side of the rails. There was an awful moment when he lay there and I thought he might have broken his neck but, when I reached him, he just looked at me with one eye as much as to say, "Here I am". He was ridden in the outdoor school later that day and was absolutely perfect.'

Murphy's progress has also been followed by Neil Brown (who bought him as a youngster and sold him on to Ann) and by the inhabitants of Drumora, the village in Co. Down, Northern Ireland where he was born. I was invited over there to give a talk to the Half Bred Horse Breeders Society in the summer of 1986 and Lady Dorinda Dunleith, the Society's chairman, very kindly arranged for me to meet Murphy's Mum and Dad.

The mare is a lovely chestnut, who is three-quarters thoroughbred and is still owned by Murphy's breeder, Jack Higgins. The stallion, Sam Brown's Royal Renown, is a quality grey thoroughbred who is smaller than I had expected at 16 hands, but has the same intelligent head as his son. He also has the same habit of bobbing his head up and down, which made the similarity between the two seem almost uncanny.

Murphy always does his head-bobbing act when we put him into the lorry and drive him to the gallops or to the hills at Castle Combe, but never when he is on his way to an event. He has everything sussed out so well that he knows the difference. When his saddle is put on before he goes in the lorry, he knows he's either going galloping or to the hills, which he enjoys as long as they're not too steep. On these occasions he head-bobs throughout the journey and then shakes from head to foot with excitement when we arrive and let down the ramp.

Murphy (whom we have nicknamed Myrtle) has always seen himself as the boss, and he believes in keeping me in my place. In his younger days he would have nothing to do with a combination fence that I tried to ride him over at home; he would simply take the bit when about six strides away and veer off to one side. I didn't feel he was frightened; he seemed to be telling me that, whatever ideas I might have, he always believed in doing his own thing.

Only once have I given him a good strong whack. That time he did

The baby Murphy competing in his first three-day event at Avenches in Switzerland

get the message and behaved quite well afterwards, but I would never wish to force the issue again. He needs to have the right attitude towards the rider, which means that I have to try and win his co-operation so that he wants to do things for me. This is the fascination of working with horses. I am continually trying to assess each individual's character, so that we can reach an understanding – and it can take a while to suss some of them out. Analysing the physical strengths and inadequacies seems to me equally important, because the whole art of training involves using the strong points and, wherever possible, overcoming the weaknesses.

I had steerage problems for quite a long time. I remember taking him to a one-day event in his first year and he went straight past two island fences. He had no objection to jumping an obstacle in a hedge that would take him into the next field, but he thought it was plain stupid to go over a fence that was sitting in the middle of a field when it was so much easier to go round it. He was simply using his head.

After he had sailed past those island fences, I pulled up and dismounted, thinking that something must have happened to his bit. I found it flapping against his cheekbone. The whole bit, including the ring on one side, had been pulled through his mouth while I had been using two hands on one rein in my fruitless efforts to steer him.

Goody four-shoes at Burghley

As his dressage improved, it became easier to keep Murphy going straight (and in the direction I wanted) across country. But we then encountered another problem. Whenever we attempted to teach him a new dressage movement, his immediate reaction was to rear. This happened when we taught him to rein back, with me on board and Dot standing in front with her hand on his chest to push him back while I gave the aids. Instead of stepping backwards, he went straight up on his hind legs.

He repeated this performance at his next event. After we had halted at 'X', Murphy began a series of rears that went on for about a minute under the slightly amused gaze of Isabel Reid, who was judging. 'I'm so glad the Holgate horses sometimes do that sort of thing as well,' Isabel said to me later.

I had not intended to rein back that day but, when we halted at 'X', something must have clicked in Murphy's mind to associate it with a lesson at home. It was the same routine with each new movement – shoulder in, half pass and all the rest. I would ask him quietly for something new and up he went on his hindlegs. Having ridden him gently round in a circle, I'd ask again, with the same result. After the third or fourth time, he did what was asked of him and there was never any further problem with that particular movement.

There were also rears, followed by angry kickbacks, whenever I leant over to pat him from the saddle. It took me a full eighteen months, plus many pocketfuls of nuts, before he would accept it without retaliating. I used to lean down to give him a handful of nuts and then pat him; after that year and a half he decided that maybe it wasn't so bad after all. But to this day he dislikes being patted while we are going across country and he shows his disapproval by flicking his ears back, as much as to say: 'Hop off'!

Everyone at Ivyleaze has some story to tell about Murphy. Dot recalls the day when she was leading him quietly along behind a row of cars at a show-jumping meeting and he spooked at something, bashed straight into her and knocked her flat on her face. She was livid with the big grey bully, who had shown such a total lack of respect that he pretended not to know she was there.

My mother talks about his performance when he sees a steep hill and thinks he might have to go up it. These sharp climbs are used as part of his fittening programme, but he loathes the thought of putting so much effort into something he finds totally boring and he starts puffing as soon as he sees them. Apparently, he puffs far more looking at the big hills than he does going up them.

Moysie Barton, who had Murphy at her place for two of his winter holidays, remembers, with great amusement, how he behaved towards the flock of sheep she shared with Hamish's mother (another Virginia). He was there during some horrendous weather, when all the animals were particularly keen on food, and the sheep made the big mistake of trying to share Murphy's supper.

'We used to see our Welsh Mountain lambs flying through the air,' she says. 'Whenever they went to Murphy's feed bin, he picked them up by the scruff of the neck with his teeth and literally hurled them out of the way. He never did them any harm, but we did start to worry in case he might get hurt by the long curly horns on the rams.'

There was no damage done, which was just as well because the sheep never learnt their lesson. Night after night, they were thrown aside by our butch Irishman.

As Nicky Ide-Smith, who looks after him, says, 'You need to know Murphy, otherwise he'd frighten the living daylights out of you with the faces he pulls. He's very soft at heart, but he feels he has to put on his big macho act. Every time I shut the stable door and walk away, I hear his

Yahoo! Murphy takes a flier at Burghley

teeth snapping behind me. He doesn't mean to get me . . . at least I don't think he does! When we take him to an event on his own, without any of the other horses from the yard, he's always as soft as could be, simply because he realizes he's getting 100 per cent attention.'

I love riding Murphy across country. He has such an enormous stride and wonderful natural jump that he feels like a Rolls-Royce. He is not as nimble as Priceless, but he is just as quick-witted and he has learnt to accommodate the size of his long body through combination fences which have short distances – while I have learnt to sit still and avoid interfering. In a show-jumping combination – with, say, one stride to the second fence and two strides to the third – I frequently see that we are going to come very close to the last element. I do nothing, except close my eyes and pray! Being a bright boy and very athletic, Murphy has learnt (without any help from me) to shorten his stride to as little as two feet so as to cope with such situations.

Help! Murphy takes off a stride early at the wide Gallows fence at Burghley

He ran in his first three-day event at Avenches in Switzerland in 1984, when he was supposedly a six-year-old, though we have since discovered

that he was, in fact, only five. Even though a year younger than we thought, he won the contest and gave a marvellous boost to my confidence as I prepared for my big date with Priceless at the Los Angeles Olympics.

The grey Irishman, whose long body makes him feel much bigger than his 16.2 hands, had a set-back the following year when we thought he was lame in his shoulder. Our vet, Don Attenburrow, literally put his finger on the problem when he touched Murphy's elbow and the horse nearly went through the roof of his stable. He had to take a rest in the fields before coming back into work for the first Audi Chatsworth three-day event that October.

The return to work may not have seemed such a good idea since I had my first fall with him at Chatsworth, where I chose to take the quick route (involving a double bounce) through the three elements of the Dog Kennels. I made the mistake of riding into it too fast for Murphy's length of stride; he landed uncomfortably close to the second element and almost into the base of the third. He just managed to clear the obstacle and stay on his feet; I just failed to stay on board and did an abrupt dive to collide headfirst with the ground. I had to learn the hard way about the right pace for Murphy at certain types of fence. We didn't meet another bounce until Weston Park in the spring of 1987 and, having approached it at a slow canter, he jumped it perfectly.

We completed the Chatsworth course (after Murphy had done some galloping on his own around the beautiful park) and, despite the hiccup, we were thrilled with him. Whatever others may have thought, the Ivyleaze group believed he had shown he had what it takes to be a top-class eventer. Some time was to elapse before he could prove it to the rest of the world.

My next big date that year was at the altar, when I married Hamish, and changed my name from Holgate to Leng. It followed a rather fraught evening during which a horrifying thought struck me as Louise Bates and I were running through the marriage service. Had we given the wedding guests the right words. Or would I come down the aisle of Badminton church to hear them singing: Here comes the bride, short, fat and wide . . .? I even phoned Louise's mother to check this out! All would then have been well had I not discovered a spot on the end of my nose, which was cheerfully pointed out to me by Louise, and I spent the next few hours fussing over it.

But the day was wonderful; I am sure I will always look back on it as the best day of my life. I will also remember, with enormous gratitude, the great efforts everyone made (in particular my mother and Dot) to make sure that everything was perfect. There were marvellous flowers, delicious food and champagne that flowed during the reception and, after all the farewells, on the car ride to London when Hamish and I drank some more out of paper cups. We were being driven by Howard from the village garage and, when we arrived in London for our wedding night, he solemnly announced that my suitcases had been left behind. He sounded so utterly convincing that I believed him ... until he opened the car boot! The following day Big Ham and I went off to Nepal, where we played Elephant Polo – a game that is probably not on most honeymooners' itinerary.

Murphy took a back seat again in the Spring of 1986, while Night Cap was being prepared for Badminton and Priceless for the World Championship at Gawler in South Australia. The grey showed no extra sign of respect for me when I returned from the other side of the world to start riding him again, but I am quite sure he knew that Nicky was getting him fit for something that was of importance to Murphy Himself. I had time for one cross-country school at Wylye before taking 'Himself' to the three-day event at Le Touquet in France.

It was there, in the process of winning with the only unpenalized cross-country round, that the Rolls-Royce description first came to mind. Isabel Reid, who had looked after me when I was on junior teams and had been judging Murphy during his rearing display in the dressage arena, was in raptures about him. There have been many other people who have told me how magnificent he looks when galloping; from on board, whatever the going may be, it feels as though he is floating across the ground.

The mechanism of his hind legs is extraordinary and can best be seen from behind as he gallops away from you. From the rear view you can see that he lifts his hocks up very high and then thrusts them forward under his stomach to punch off for the next stride. I have never before ridden a horse with that sort of gallop.

Le Touquet had the equivalent of a small advanced course, so I was well aware that Murphy's next three-day event at Burghley a few months later would ask some far more serious questions. I took him to five one-day events beforehand, anxious that he should gain as much experience as possible and equally anxious to make sure that I knew him as well as I could. The time spent in Australia had made it a difficult year for getting properly acquainted with any of the horses apart from Priceless (whom I knew rather well anyway) and I felt that I needed to know much more about Murphy before we encountered our first really big test together.

Because of his wonderful action, Murphy's dressage has always been good – even though he regards it as boring. I only worked him in for twenty-five minutes before he was due to do his test at Burghley, but that seemed more than enough to him. He must have thought that the boring work was over and was no doubt looking forward to the pleasant prospect

The Silver Buckle coffin at Burghley, where Murphy made his own unique adjustment to get his hocks underneath him for the first element. Having jumped off all fours, he is about to put his hind feet down to punch off over the fence. He jumped the second element in more orthodox style, putting his weight on his fore-legs and then bringing his hind legs forward (as is about to happen in the second frame) for a normal take-off. He used his special adjustment again at the final element of returning to his temporary stable, until I pulled him up beside my mother and put on the top hat and tails she had been holding in readiness. Murphy understood the significance of this and, realizing that there was more dressage to come, he gave an enormous sigh.

But he is a nice enough character to make an effort for me and he did a very good test. My mother's brother, Jack Rice, who has always given me such wonderful support, told me later that he had never seen a horse try as hard as Murphy did in the dressage arena in Burghley. It helped that we had a big audience, which was quite a surprise since we were doing our test in the early morning; Murphy always has a much greater sense of purpose when there are plenty of people around to watch him perform. At the end of the two days of dressage, we held the lead with a marginal advantage of 0.8 of a penalty.

Anyone passing through the Burghley stables on the Friday, Saturday or Sunday morning might have been surprised to see a large grey horse stretched flat out on his bed of shavings, fast asleep. Murphy must have realized that he was at a three-day event and decided that he needed plenty of rest in preparation for the strenuous efforts ahead.

He is not nearly as sensible about conserving his strength on the roads and tracks. Whereas Priceless always used as little energy as possible on those two sections (A and C) of the speed, endurance and cross-country test, Murphy puts a great deal of wasted effort into spooking at pretty well anything we happen to pass. He does much the same out hacking, but it becomes an extra special performance at a three-day event.

At Burghley, he spooked at every shadow, flower, bird, human, drain-pipe and whatever else caught his attention on the roads and tracks; they all became goblins that were about to attack him. In between these sections, he whizzed happily around the steeplechase course. This is not my favourite part of the three-day event; I am always glad to have it safely behind me because I know how easy it is to make a silly mistake there, before even reaching the cross-country.

Murphy was still as strong as a lion when we set out to tackle the twenty-eight cross-country fences on phase D, the vital section of the test. The Malting's Rails and Wall (fences 20 and 21) had bothered me most on the walk round and I had spent about four hours there with Dot and Nicky McIrvine trying to decide which route I would take. I had gone the fast way – over the rails and straight on over the corner of walls – with Priceless the previous year when Burghley staged the European Championships. But on that occasion I had the benefit of many previous years' experience with Priceless; I knew him well and trusted him to keep the essential straight line.

On the other hand Murphy was a newcomer to the big event, the first young horse I had taken to Burghley for six years. Did I dare to risk the time-saving corner or should I play safe and take the slow alternative? I decided that if he were straight and accurate over the preceding nineteen fences, jumping exactly where I asked each time, it would be worth having a go at the difficult corner.

He gave me supreme confidence over the first eighteen fences. As soon as he saw each obstacle he made his own adjustments, switching his weight back onto his hocks in preparation to jump. All I needed to do was to sit up and think about where to take off. I then made a real hash of the nineteenth fence, with its uninviting name of the Gallows. I saw a long stride as we came down towards it; then told myself I was a twit even to think of taking off so far away from such a wide fence – so I sat still. Murphy took off regardless and I was left floundering. This slightly unnerved me; I didn't want the horse to think that I would fail to go forward with him at the next two crucial obstacles.

We went for the Malting's Wall Corner nevertheless, with my stick switched to my left hand and held against his shoulder to discourage him from running out to that side. As we landed over the rails, I hooked back for five strides to the corner of walls and came in uncomfortably close to it; Murphy had to really balloon to get over. It was a brave and honest effort because he could so easily have ducked out to the left. In retrospect I realize that I should have gone on four strides; I saw two horses jump the corner on four later that day and they did it easily. But I was not anxious to be the first to prove that it could be done!

After the Weir at fence 24, Murphy took off with me. He was simply flying on that great long stride of his and I was enormously thankful that he had become such a careful jumper; there were four fences left and he slowed as he came to each one so that he could get back on his hocks and jump it safely. He was pulling like a train as we went through the finish, showing no hint of fatigue after covering a total of 22.26 kilometres (nearly 14 miles).

We saw blood in his mouth after he had finished and thought that he must have bitten his tongue. Closer investigation revealed a large deep hole on the upper bar of his mouth where an abscess, which we had failed to spot because it was so far back, had burst. The straight mouthpiece of his Kimblewick bit could have been touching that spot and he may have been running away from pain on the last part of the cross-country.

We switched to a rubber snaffle for the show jumping; its nutcracker action put the pressure on a different part of the bars of his mouth, leaving the wound untouched. I have no problem in holding him over a show-jumping course so I was perfectly happy to be using a milder bit – and he was in brilliant form. I have never known him to practice jump so well; he felt very much like Priceless as we prepared for the final test.

Normally Murphy finds the show jumping at a one-day event rather boring. But the parade at Burghley – the bands, the crowds and the clapping – gave him a great lift; he really sparkled as he went in to jump the necessary clear round for victory. Less than a fence behind us were Bruce Davidson on J.J. Babu and Richard Walker on Accumulator, who were also among the ten to finish without anything to add to their dressage scores. The slender advantage we had gained in the dressage, when Murphy had been trying so hard for me, had made all the difference.

I would have loved to see how Murphy reacted to Badminton the following spring but I never had the chance. Nor did I have an opportunity of riding him at any other three-day event during 1987. He was due to start canter work in preparation for the European Championships when he struck the side of his off-fore tendon while galloping out in the field. In the knowledge that bruising takes a long time to heel, we decided to rest him for the remainder of the season.

Below: *Home and dry, with Murphy's round at King's Somborne recorded on video*

Right: *Murphy jumped a wonderful clear round to clinch victory at Burghley, 1986*

CHAPTER FOUR

Good-looking Athlete

Master Craftsman is the apple of my mother's eye. 'He's the best of the lot,' she says, whenever his name is mentioned.

He is also a favourite with Hamish, mainly as the result of a weekend with just my mother and myself at Belton Park, where I rode Crafty in his first advanced class in the spring of 1987. We had not taken a groom (and Dot was away with the girls at another event) so Ham, who likes to be occupied, decided this was the time to get involved. He mucked out the stables, gave Crafty his hay-net, put boots on the horse for the show jumping and so on. He enjoyed it much more than standing around and we, of course, were delighted to have some help! Since Belton, Ham feels a greater sense of relationship with Crafty than with any of the other horses.

My mother always extols Master Craftsman's virtues with greater emphasis when I am around. She reckons that I fail to appreciate this good-looking thoroughbred son of Master Spiritus, whom she bought as a three-year-old. She went to see him in Somerset after receiving a phone call to say that he was for sale. Mark Todd, who was then living in the next village and was a fairly frequent visitor, happened to be around so she persuaded him to go along with her.

Master Craftsman's first advanced one-day event at Belton Park, which was an exciting day because it proved he had potential

Crafty was out in a field that had sundry pieces of equipment in it – my mother thinks there were barrels and bits of wood; there may have been a roller. It is not quite what our horses are used to, but she realized that this youngster had already learnt to keep a good look-out as to where he put his feet. He is out of a Deep Run mare, which would mean a great deal in the racing world but didn't impress my mother in the least. She was equally unimpressed by the sire, who had died in 1980. Though the progeny of Master Spiritus (which includes Mark Phillips's Cartier and Robert Lemieux's The Gamesmaster) have since made the stallion's name much better known in eventing, it meant very little at the time when she first saw Crafty.

My mother reacts to horses as she does to people; there are some she likes instantly, but she couldn't really tell you why. She says that the horse's 'overall appearance has to appeal' and that she looks at its 'attitude to life' – which is not a great deal of help for anyone who would like to follow her method of picking future winners. Her father had the same sure and instinctive gift for buying good horses, and he could not have analysed it either.

In Master Craftsman's case, my mother may have been influenced by the resemblance to another dark-brown thoroughbred she had bought as a yearling back in 1969. This was Tio Pepe, the most infuriating horse I

Crafty and his minder, Nicky Ide-Smith

Ben Hovis (*left*) and Welton Chit Chat with my mother, Dot and myself, plus two-thirds of the Ivyleaze pack

Master Craftsman attacking the big advanced course at King's Somborne

Mandy Hosp with two of her charges, Freeway (*left*) and Beneficial

Murphy's chestnut mother with another of her offspring

Badminton 1986. Having run out once, Night Cap proves he can jump this fence as I ride him on a straight line

Private Rose (Smartie) taking time off in the field at home

Below: The British Airways Elephant Polo team. Left
to right: Concorde pilot Colin Morris, Hamish, Lucinda
Green, Ellie and her driver, myself and David Green

It's true that horses can fly – just look at Murphy!

Having been very strong coming down the hill, Murphy jumps the difficult second last fence at King's Somborne, 1987

Who's a pretty boy?

Smiley Begorrah shows that where there's a will there's a way

Murphy Himself at Stowell Park, 1987

Cupboard love from Master Craftsman

Ballyhack is eager to attack one of his first novice courses

Master Craftsman shows style and confidence at Downton Castle

have ever met. He had the most uncanny knack of catching you unawares, whether treading on your toes (and always contriving to catch you twice, with both a fore and hind foot) or flinging his empty water bucket to hit you with an aim that never failed. If you were picking up droppings in his stable, he would tip the basket over as soon as your back was turned.

'I loved that horse very dearly and I suppose Crafty did remind me of him,' says my mother. I was less enamoured of the infuriating Tio Pepe, which may have been part of the reason why it took me a long time to appreciate this new thoroughbred, even though he is very laid back and easy-going.

He is 16.3 hands and feels bigger; I thought he was too big for me and that we would never hit it off together. Like Murphy, he is very long and it seemed difficult to get his two ends connected when I first rode him. Dot deserves all the credit for making him more co-ordinated. She is brilliant with young horses on the lunge and she did a vast amount of work with Crafty, often lunging him over poles which helped to connect the two ends and produced a little more elevation in his trot.

'His parents were bred to race and going forward is his thing,' says Dot. 'He's not too keen on being told to turn away and do a circle; he finds it quite difficult mentally to get himself into gear for that.'

His breeding also meant that he jumped like a racehorse; he always wanted to fly his fences, taking off from a long way back and throwing a long scopey jump. I thought that was the way he would always be; it came so naturally for him to jump like a hurdler. We wanted him to use his scope while containing it, learning to shorten and jump in a more rounded way.

Novice events did not seem to be doing him much good. He went round them in his own hurdling style, which was adequate for clearing small fences but never made me feel that I had a potential three-day star in the making. Thinking I was never going to click with him, I suggested to my mother that he should be sold. She would have none of it. 'You keep him and see how he goes in intermediates,' she said, determined not to part with her dark-brown favourite.

So Master Craftsman and I did our first joint intermediate event in August 1986 at Dauntsey, where he suddenly started to think about what he was doing. The higher the fences became, the more he respected them and learnt to round his back. He did a total of four intermediates that autumn and was always in the first five placings.

I was beginning to feel more at home on him, but still had my doubts as to whether we would ever be quite right for each other. By now there were people who thought he would be exactly right for them. Large sums of money were offered for the handsome thoroughbred and I still

wondered whether it would be better to sell him. But my mother was determined to keep Crafty and I knew, on past form, that her instinct could well be right.

It was partly to help me find a more positive attitude that we took him to the French three-day event at le Lion d'Angers in October 1986, after Murphy had been to Burghley and Night Cap to Poland. It was his first three-day event and he took it all in his stride – with a really pleasing dressage test, a clear round over the cross-country course (which was of intermediate standard) and another clear in the show jumping. Remarkably, he finished in fourth place with the best of the three British scores. My own feelings and my mother's instinct were now in complete accord!

Master Craftsman has the most remarkable temperament. Whereas so many thoroughbreds become hopelessly dizzy when they get excited, he is totally unflappable. Though he has his moments of aggression towards other horses, he loves people and is never happier than when he has human company.

When I was asked to do a television commercial for Oil of Ulay, I had no hesitation in choosing Crafty for the galloping horse scene. He was the

Left: Master Craftsman at Weston Park

Below: Crafty took to the Bicton advanced course like a duck to water

only one who could be relied on to keep his cool under any circumstances; nothing ever bothers him. It was to prove quite a test of his equanimity, but he came through it with flying colours.

For the opening scene, which was shot at The Watley Manor near Malmesbury, we had to canter at a fair lick along a wide grass verge that ran through an avenue of trees. Diagonally ahead of us, being driven on the road, was a truck carrying a huge camera and about ten people, and we had to stay within a couple of yards of it. Most young horses would regard this as a terribly alarming exercise, but not Master Craftsman. In true Hollywood style, we had to go through this routine about eight times and the horse was happy to oblige, with his ears pricked forward for each sharp spin, along the verge.

Enormous quantities of food were consumed before and after filming. We had breakfast soon after I arrived, when I would have much preferred to get on with the job in hand, and lunch came immediately afterwards. Both were served from an enormous catering van that contained an unbelievable array of food, with hot and cold dishes of amazing variety.

Master Craftsman was not quite so eager to oblige for the stable scene, when he was supposed to have his head out over the door while I stood outside. He was less than enthusiastic about the large silver screen that had been erected outside the stable to reflect the sun back on us and preferred to stay at the rear of his box. Wendy, who used to be part of our team, eventually solved the problem by leaning with all her might against his rear end to keep his head over the door for about half an hour, until the scene was completed.

There was also a scene in front of the dressing table at nearby Luckington Court, a lovely old house belonging to Mrs Horn who has followed the eventing scene for many years. It was her husband, Colonel Trevor Horn, who was the first director and course designer of the Badminton Three-Day Event when it began back in 1949.

Fortunately, she seemed in no hurry to get rid of us. It was to take an awful long time to get this scene right, because I seemed incapable of the simple task I had been set. I was supposed to apply a dab of Oil of Ulay on my cheek and then rub it in with two circles of my middle fingers; if it took three circles to disappear we would over-run the allotted time. I was enormously impressed by the professionalism that insisted on every-thing being technically perfect and only wished that I could have been more slick. I have no problems with putting the stuff on my face at home, but that particular day the oil went in my eye, up my nose and in my hair. When I did manage to keep it on my cheek, I succeeded in missing a small part of it with those two circles. Each time I failed, I had to have attention from the make-up lady before we tried again. Everyone was wonderfully patient and eventually – at about the fifteenth attempt – I actually achieved what was required of me.

I am pleased to say that the speaking parts went much better. Two introductions had to be recorded later in London, one each for the seventeen and twenty-second commercials, and I enjoyed trying to fit my words into exactly the right time. I was a little anxious while watching the commercial breaks on television after it was all completed, but I have only seen the advert once and, to my relief, I didn't think it was too bad.

By then we were considering Master Craftsman's future in eventing. When I began riding him after the winter break, he felt like the most mature seven-year-old I had ever known. He had always been sensible, with more of a pony brain than that of a flighty thoroughbred, but now he was also learning to adapt himself to a sport that was foreign to his breeding. He knew the ropes and understood exactly what was coming up as soon as he saw the dressage arena, the show jumping or the start of the cross-country.

Nicky, who looks after Crafty as well as Night Cap and Murphy, also noticed a change. 'He's developing into a real character, it's almost as though he's been talking to other event horses and feels that he should be big and butch as well,' she said. 'He's basically very sweet, but he now threatens to bite me when I'm grooming him. Then he looks at me as if to say: "I know I'm one of the big boys now and I've got to act like them, but I'm not sure whether that was quite the right way to do it".'

Crafty's first event in the spring of 1987 was at Weston Park, where he jumped well over a fair-sized intermediate track. He then did his first advanced *hors concours* at Belton, where he showed his appreciation of Hamish's efforts as groom by taking the bigger fences in his stride. He would have finished tenth, which we felt was a fine achievement for a horse that had only been jumping in novices twelve months earlier.

His jumping was improving all the time, as I again appreciated when I took him to a cross-country school at Wylye, where David Green now administers the schooling sessions and trains some of his own pupils. I had taken all the older horses there when Lord and Lady Hugh Russell were still in residence and it felt distinctly odd to be jumping on those windswept hills of Salisbury Plain without Lady Hugh's usual vocal accompaniment. I half expected her to appear over the hill, in full voice, behind the wheel of her famous mini-moke.

How I wished she had still been there to scream at me! She would have spotted any slight deviation off a straight line; now I had to be grown up and work it out for myself. I still phone her quite often to ask for advice, especially when we have been discussing the future plans for one of our horses and I feel an outside opinion might help. We were slightly dithering over whether we should take Master Craftsman to the Swedish three-day event that was held in Stockholm; Lady Hugh probably helped us to make a firm decision by saying that she thought he should go.

Though still only seven, he felt ready for the challenge. His whole balance had changed since the previous year – partly by schooling but also through his own mental attitude. He had realized that he needed to get his quarters engaged and his back rounded when jumping a fence. He then found it easy, as he proved with two lovely clear rounds in a Grade C show-jumping class at Larkhill, where the last parallel was over five feet. Hamish was on hand that day to record the performance on our video camera. He has become quite a dab hand at this and it is obviously a great help for me to have the chance of seeing whether I'm over-checking the horse, or whatever. After Larkhill, Crafty was also clear over big advanced one-day event tracks at Stowell Park and King's Somborne.

We had the benefit of Pat Burgess's help with our show jumping before going to Stockholm where I was hoping that Crafty would jump clear. Since he was only seven (which made him the youngest horse in the entire competition) I could hardly wish for more. But he exceeded these expectations magnificently, showing a maturity far beyond his years.

Thanks to his equable temperament, he took not the slightest notice of the torrential rain that fell while we did our dressage test and he was lying fourth as we went into the cross-country. I had no intention of pushing him, but I did choose one difficult line through a combination of bounces because I wanted him to prove to me that he could use his brain and be athletic. He gave me a superb ride and, though we weren't hurrying, we had slipped back by only one place to fifth at the end of the day.

I would have been more than happy to settle for fifth prize. I never dreamt that Crafty's clear show jumping round would eventually move us up to second place below Bruce Davidson who won the individual for the United States on J. J. Babu. Master Craftsman also contributed to a victory for the British team, which included Lucinda Green on Shannagh, Rachel Hunt on Friday Fox and Jon Evans on The Cordwainer.

One particularly happy passenger was on the flight from Stockholm to Heathrow soon after the awards were presented. I had to miss out on the celebrations because a helicopter was to take the winning Derby jockey, Steve Cauthen, and myself from Heathrow to Alton Towers for the dinner that preceded Prince Edward's fund-raising version of 'It's a Knock-Out'.

Having changed into evening wear at the heliport, I hoped there was no lingering smell of horses when I met up with Hamish among the most amazing assembly of royalty and superstars.

I had the honour to be on the Princess Royal's Save the Children Fund team, listed in the programme in alphabetical order: Jenny Agutter, Anthony Andrews, Sheena Easton, Deborah Flintoff, Sunil Gavaskar, Emlyn Hughes, Tom Jones, a certain Virginia Leng, Walter Payton and Cliff Richard. And such was our enthusiasm to win for our Royal leader that I came close to losing an important item of clothing during the final game in which I was carried away by a dashing knight – Anthony Andrews. There was a nasty ripping sound as a maiden (yours truly) was flung onto the knight's wooden steed and it was heaved into rapid motion by members of our team. The whole of my skirt's waistband was torn apart but fortunately the front section remained intact. The maiden may have looked dishevelled but at least she was decent!

We were overjoyed to have won for the Princess Royal, who had shown such wonderful comradeship and sense of fun. After that it was

Crafty keeps his ears pricked despite the downpour in Sweden, showing his good temperament

Left: *Bruce Davidson (USA) was pleased to win again with his indomitable J. J. Babu and I was thrilled to be second*

Below: *An escort in Sweden for the leading woman rider (myself on Master Craftsman) and the top Swedish man*

back to real live horses at Ivyleaze, where Master Craftsman had begun to think of himself as an elegant showman, giving his own one-horse act when out in the field by flying rounds in circles. Dot witnessed one of these performances.

'I was teaching in the arena and I saw him getting up quite a good speed for the size of paddock,' she said. 'His rug was hanging down like a necklace and his leg straps were trailing when I realized that he was going to jump out. He came diagonally over the white railings and then disappeared from my sight. I gave the loudest scream I could muster and Elaine came racing out of the yard; fortunately she's been here long enough to know the difference between my shouts and my screams! She caught him while he was doing a circle of the lawn.'

By now I not only appreciated Crafty's ability, but had begun to feel at one with him. I remember waking up in the night and thinking about both Crafty and Murphy; it then dawned on me that they were the first very fast, long-striding horses I had ever ridden. I needed to recognize that it was the start of a new era; I would have to learn how to adapt to a different experience. Suddenly it seemed an exciting challenge.

The winning British team at the Stockholm Three-Day event in Sweden with chef d'équipe Lord Patrick Beresford. Left to right: Rachel Hunt on Friday Fox, Lucinda Green on Shannagh, myself on Master Craftsman and Jon Evans on The Cordwainer

CHAPTER FIVE

The Clown and the Shy Boy

Though we seemed to have been on the move for most of 1986, we still leapt at the chance of a November trip to Ireland. I had been asked there to judge the Golden Saddle award that is sponsored by Spillers; my mother and Dot decided to come with me and indulge their obsession for buying (or at least looking at) horses. Since almost every horse in Ireland is for sale, this is the happiest of hunting grounds for both of them.

We stopped at Chester on our way to catch the night sailing from Liverpool to Dublin. Dot and I had never seen this lovely old walled city before and, for once in my life, I had a really good excuse to do some shopping because I was due to go to Buckingham Palace ten days later to receive the MBE. So I was able to buy myself a red dress and black, cossack-style David Fox hat in Chester without too many twinges of guilt over the money I was spending.

We then had dinner with John Stone, the marketing manager of Spillers, who was travelling with us to Ireland. Having lingered over our delicious food, we needed to do the last lap of the journey to Liverpool at high speed; we were therefore none too pleased when we saw people waving at us urgently from the hard shoulder of the motorway, obviously intent on slowing us down. It was just as well they did restrain us, since a large herd of cows was heading down the motorway just ahead of us.

Both Ballyhack and I enjoyed ourselves when we had our first cross country school together at Badgworth

We arrived in the nick of time at Liverpool harbour, where our car was the last one allowed onto the boat. I then spent a sleepless night, feeling claustrophobic in the cabin and petrified of the rough sea which sent waves slapping ferociously against the porthole.

The annual Golden Saddle awards have been going for the last ten years and are given, after about half a dozen assessment days and a final, to any rider in Ireland who shows true potential in dressage, show jumping or eventing. I had been asked to help in judging the 1986 final, which took place at Iris Kellet's wonderful riding school at Kill in Co. Dublin on the day we arrived in Ireland, feeling far from rested after a night in the tossing cabin. The eventing 'golden saddle' (a bursary of up to £800 to be used for training) was awarded to Amanda Lilley from Northern Ireland, who has since spent a fortnight with us at Ivyleaze.

One of my fellow judges was the Irish show jumper, Con Power. When he heard that we wanted to stay on in Ireland for a couple of days and look at some horses, he very kindly put us in touch with a farmer friend of his in Co. Wexford called Noel Roche – and we drove south the following day to meet him.

Noel came with us in the car, which Dot was driving along country roads that were quiet except for the squealing of brakes when our guide

Ballyhack becoming bolder by the minute at Twesledown

gave a sudden instruction: 'Stop here and back up. There might be a horse for sale in the farm we've just passed.'

As my mother says: 'It could only happen in Ireland.' No wonder she feels so much at home there!

It was on one of those stops that we came to Claire Day's yard and found a five-year-old bay, who was then called Jack Striker. We were being shown another horse, but my mother always believes in taking a look into the rest of the stables and Jack, who was in one of them, took her fancy. He was due to be shown as a potential show jumper to some Italians, but they had been diverted.

Dot also liked the young bay. 'He reminds me very much of Priceless as a five-year-old,' she said.

Ballyhack (Jack) eats everything in sight, including flowers and plants

It may have been rather mean to remind her that she hadn't liked P when she first saw him at that age, but she took it in good part and countered, with a huge smile, 'I like to think that I've learnt a few things in the last nine years.'

Claire had just been working the horse, but she agreed to get on him again so that we could see how he went for her. Then I had a ride – and was also reminded of the young Priceless. Needless to say, we said that we would like to buy Jack subject to a satisfactory report from Don Attenburrow.

Looking back we realize how lucky we were to have had Noel as our guide; he was liked and respected by all the local farmers and therefore he made it possible for us to see the best horses in Co. Wexford. Apparently you only get to see the worst ones if you are taken around by someone the farmers dislike – as, we were told, happens regularly to one leading international rider.

Having thanked our splendid guide, the Ivyleaze trio set off for dinner in Waterford, driving through fabulous scenery to catch the ferry at Ballyhack.

'It was like going back in time,' says Dot, recalling the wooden platform which carried the three of us and the car across the estuary of the River Suir and into Co. Waterford. Dot drove onto the floating platform as reluctantly as if it had been a mine field and her face was ashen as we crossed the stretch of water.

Because Dot had made the ferry crossing so memorable, we decided to call the new horse Ballyhack. Perhaps we should have given it more careful consideration; when I mentioned his name at a press conference for the first time, one of the journalists asked: 'You're not getting at us by any chance?' Until then it had not even occurred to me that it could have the slightest connection with someone who writes for a newspaper!

We had a phone call from Neil Brown, Murphy's previous owner, shortly after our return from Ireland. He said that he had a nice young horse at his place in Northern Ireland that he thought would interest us. Would we like to see it? My mother would not normally hold back, but it so happened that she and Dot (the two intrepid travellers) were about to go to Australia for a well-earned holiday with David and Jenny Malcolm, whom we had first met about twenty years earlier in the Philippines.

Before leaving my mother made careful plans which I was supposed to put into practice. I was to take an early flight to Dublin on the appointed day and would meet up with Neil, who was driving his horse to the airport. Ballyhack would also be there, having been driven up from Co. Wexford. I was to find somewhere near the airport where I could ride Neil's horse, Money Broker. Then I would return to the airport and meet Don Attenburrow, who was flying in from Bristol. We would need to find some suitable place where Ballyhack and Money Broker (assuming that I liked him) could be vetted, then Don and I would take our separate

Money Broker at his first event, the pre-novice at Wylye

flights back to England.

'Thanks a million,' I said. 'I think I'd rather do *The Krypton Factor* again!'

A few days before my mother left for Australia, she and Uncle Jack came with me to Buckingham Palace where I was to receive the insignia of my MBE. Hamish would have loved to be there, but he insisted that Uncle Jack should come with me instead because he had contributed so much to my riding career.

The instructions given to MBEs were not quite as complicated as those for my forthcoming visit to Dublin, but I was anxious to get them right and I kept running through them in my head while the Lords, Dames and OBEs went ahead of us. I was to walk forward, turn, curtsy, walk forward another four steps and then bend forward, while her majesty pinned the insignia on my dress.

When the time for bending forward came, I found myself face to face with the most beautiful sapphire I have ever seen. It was on a brooch, surrounded by diamonds, and set off quite perfectly against the Queen's pale blue dress. I felt as though my own eyes were sparkling from the reflection as I stood upright again.

The Queen said that I had two lovely horses and they had both been very successful. 'Thank you, Ma'am, but this is by far the greatest honour,' I replied.

Remembering the instructions I then shook hands, moved back four paces, curtsied and moved away. We were to have a celebratory lunch, but it took some time for us to find the restaurant because Uncle Jack and I had a difference of opinion as to which of the two St James' Streets it was in – and, needless to say, we went to the wrong one. In the end I caught a taxi, leaving Uncle Jack to deal with the problems of parking the car. Hamish and our guests were already waiting at the restaurant. They included his mother and brother, Louise Bates and Dorothy. We wondered why Hamish's best man, Johnnie Gorman, had not turned up – until it was discovered that I had given him the wrong date.

A week or so later I caught my early flight to Dublin. Hostesses and fellow passengers looked me up and down in some surprise; I had a distinct impression that they had never seen anyone boarding a plane before in anorak, jodhpurs, leather chaps and jodhpur boots, with a riding hat stuck under her arm!

Rain was lashing down as I went into the car park at Dublin airport to find Claire Day's husband, with a van and trailer containing Ballyhack, and Neil Brown in a horsebox with Money Broker. So far so good, I thought.

'We'll have to go and find a field,' I said to Neil.

Not a British Telecom engineer, but yours truly during the Krypton Factor

So, having told Ballyhack's minder that we would be half an hour or so, we set off in the horsebox.

After a few silent moments of thought, Neil said, 'I know a man a couple of miles down the road who has an outdoor arena.'

I was a bit doubtful. 'You don't imagine he'd appreciate us turning up out of the blue?'

'No problem,' said Neil, quite rightly as it turned out. The man with the arena treated this unexpected arrival of two people and a horse as though it were an everyday occurrence.

The arena contained a few jumps and was therefore ideal for my purposes. I liked the look of Money Broker when Neil rode him and I was equally pleased when I got aboard myself. There would definitely be two horses for Don to vet.

Our kind host spared us the problem of looking for a suitable place to do the vetting by saying that we were welcome to come back and use his arena again. So off we went to meet Don off his flight. He was due to arrive at 11.45 a.m. and was booked onto a return flight leaving at 3.45 p.m. We knew that there would not be much time to spare but, now that everything was going so smoothly, the whole expedition suddenly seemed feasible.

The first snag emerged when we learnt that Don's flight had been delayed by fog. It was 2.30 p.m. by the time he arrived, with all his equipment, leaving him with just an hour to vet both horses before catching his return flight to Bristol. We would have to move smartly, we agreed, and promptly ran into our second snag.

Neil, who had decided it would save time if he went on ahead of us in the horsebox, had driven into one of the airport's traffic signs and knocked it down. The police arrived and, having made the unexpected discovery that there were two vehicles in the airport, each with a horse inside, they asked endless questions while precious minutes ticked by.

Eventually both horses were vetted in the rain that bucketed down all day – and both passed Don's exhaustive examination, which included testing their wind with a radio stethoscope he had lugged with him to Ireland. Then, as we returned the horses to their vehicles, we saw Don's plane climbing into the sky above our heads. The later flight to Bristol proved to be fully booked, so our poor vet was stranded in Dublin for the night while I had to take my flight back to London. I had looked odd enough on the outward flight, but that was nothing compared with the drowned rat who sat and steamed throughout the return journey.

Collecting the two horses from Fishguard harbour a few weeks later should have been a much simpler operation – but it, too, had its problems when the boat was delayed because of rough weather. Elaine and I had been waiting to go and collect them in the lorry; the call eventually came at 7 p.m. one evening to say that the boat had sailed and would be arriving at 2 a.m. We groaned as we ran around to get ready for the journey.

It was not, to put it mildly, the easiest of drives once we had left the motorway; having steered the lorry through the winding roads of West Wales, I felt ready to sleep for a week.

'We must have some rest,' I said to Elaine, when we arrived at Fishguard. So we set the alarm for 2 a.m. and both had an hour's sleep before the clock's insistent call dragged us back to thoughts of ships and horses. There was no sign of the boat as yet, so we had time to splash cold water on our sleepy faces and drink some strong steaming coffee. Having woken ourselves up, we then discovered that the boat was late and would not be arriving until 4 a.m. I cannot recall my exact words on hearing this news, but they would probably have been unprintable.

The same is true of another occasion when I had been driving the lorry. I succeeded in getting it firmly wedged in the gateway at Urchinwood Manor Equestrian Centre, where we sometimes take the horses for school-ing, and could neither move forward nor back. My humiliation was

With my MBE and the two people who made it possible, my mother and Uncle Jack

complete when one of the farmworkers climbed into the cab and extricated it, while I examined the damage I had done. Our smart lorry had a dent and scratches all down one side.

On the Fishguard trip, we were waiting to meet Noel Roche (our guide in Co. Wexford) who had agreed to bring the two horses over by boat. He was due to return with his lorry the same day but, when he finally arrived, he told us there had been a mix-up in the booking; he was therefore in the same predicament as Don had been in Dublin. Having switched the horses into one lorry, I once again set off for home with the guilty feeling of having left someone stranded.

The two Irish youngsters, both five-year-old bays of 16.1 hands, were left to settle into their new stables, while I ate the biggest breakfast that has ever been seen and then went to bed. Though they answer to the same description, the two horses are completely different in character – as I was to discover when I rode them at home for the first time the following day.

Money Broker was unsure of himself, but eager to co-operate. Bally-hack had a mind of his own and he produced the most incredible display of fireworks as soon as I put my foot in the stirrup. I was getting on from the mounting block and was fortunately able to get my leg over his back as he let rip, bucking like no horse I had been on before. The explosions went on for about five frightening minutes, then he shot off around the arena at such speed that I felt he was bound to jump out over the rails. Eventually he came to a halt and, as though the fireworks had never happened, began behaving like a normal horse.

The following day, I was given a leg up and he was fine. But the next time I tried getting on from the mounting block, he went berserk again. Looking back to the last time I had ridden him in Ireland, when Don was testing his wind, I recalled Claire Day's husband saying that he would lead Ballyhack round for a little while before I got on.

'Is there a problem?' I had asked.

'Not really,' he said, 'the horse just has a little bit of a cold back.'

He had then legged me up and, though I could feel his back humping slightly when I reached the saddle, there was no hint of the rodeo act he performed at Ivyleaze. I also remembered that Claire had been working the horse before I had my first ride on him in Co. Wexford.

I was still wondering how to solve this problem when my mother and Dot returned from Australia, with many happy tales to tell – including, of all things, their first visit to a rock concert. Mike and Angie Rutherford, who have remained firm friends since I first met them on a holiday in Greece in 1979, had been in Australia at the same time. Mike is part of Genesis, who were then on tour in Australia, so he invited Dot (who is very much into classical music) and my mother (who is not really into music of any kind) to one of his concerts. To my great amazement, they loved every moment of it.

Needless to say, they were both anxious to see the new horses, in particular the self-effacing Money Broker. They liked the shy boy on sight and were still pleased by the clown.

'He has charisma,' Dot said of Ballyhack.

He also had a nasty habit of going berserk whenever I put my foot in the stirrup to get on him. We would somehow have to find a cure for this particular act, so we devised a plan whereby three people would stand beside him while I mounted – one of them holding his bridle and another holding the offside stirrup. It took about six weeks (during which time the girls were also getting on and off him in his stable) before I could get aboard on my own without any trouble.

Though less hairy than his rodeo act, Ballyhack's jumping was not without its problems. He used to hook off about ten strides from the fence, then get in very close and ping over it. In time he began to settle to the rein and listen, though he still has the odd moment when he decides to do his own thing and revert to the old method.

'Fine,' I say, 'it's your problem.'

The next time I come to a fence, he'll settle again. The odd lapse is just to remind me that he has ideas of his own.

Dressage is definitely not his favourite thing. On the whole, it is much too much like hard work and therefore incredibly boring. Each time we try to teach him a new movement, he starts off by saying: This is much too difficult, I can't possibly do it. I had the usual reaction when I first asked him to do lengthening trot. Impossible, he said, before eventually discovering that he could do it after all. Having decided that this was very clever, he would do nothing else but lengthening trot for weeks afterwards.

Dot, who lunges all the horses, says that Ballyhack is like a bright child who hasn't been disciplined. 'He's forever saying: I won't do this, and I shan't do that. He is also a bit of a con man, pretending to be nervous and frightened when he is nothing of the kind.'

I have vivid recollections of one of those latter occasions, which tend to occur when he is feeling rather sharp and excited. We had taken him to Newbury, for one of his first events, and I was holding him when he pretended to be frightened out of his wits by Elaine, who had just taken a quiet little jump from the step of the horsebox onto the ground. He promptly snatched the reins out of my hand and set off at full gallop.

Having caught him, he did a nice clear round on the cross-country, which should have given him the chance to let off any remaining steam. But he still had a trick up his sleeve; as Elaine was leading him back to the lorry he suddenly decided that he didn't want to go that way. So he stopped, pulled back and reared, for no reason apart from his own whim.

Ballyhack is the closest type we have to Priceless, who also liked to remind us who was boss. He has the same quick brain; he is bold and clever across country, with great confidence in his own jumping ability. I only hope we can channel his cocky sense of independence in the right direction.

Money Broker was much more like Night Cap. He was so anxious to please that he almost fell over when I patted or praised him, he was so surprised and thrilled. He now has a good home with a young rider who will take him to Pony Club competitions before they start novice one-day events together.

Sapperhill, who replaced Money Broker, is a totally different character. This 15.2hh grey, bred by Louise Bates who still owns him, has tremendous talent – and, as I discovered to my cost, a dangerous pair of hind feet. I was with him at a show in Bristol during July 1987, and was delighted with his clear show-jumping round.

Having watched some horses and carriages go past, Sapperhill was fairly wound up as we prepared for the journey home at the end of a hot and (so far) happy day. I went down the steps of the lorry to where he was tied up, approached his shoulder and ran my hand along his back to his rump, before standing close behind him to adjust his tail bandage. I had been there for no more than five seconds when he suddenly moved forward and lashed out at me, landing his hind feet on my stomach and hip.

I had to go into hospital to check that no serious internal damage had been done – and fortunately all was well. I still regard Sapperhill as a really exciting prospect for eventing but you won't catch me within range of his hind legs again!

CHAPTER SIX

The Rest of the Team

Mandy Hosp joined us in September 1986. She was not totally new to the place, having been here for lessons with Dot, who is a freelance instructor as well as an essential member of the Ivyleaze team. Mandy was then riding for other owners but, for one reason or another, she suddenly found herself short of mounts.

At about the same time, my mother was asking herself and the rest of us how we could best put something back into the sport. The idea of training a new rider gradually emerged as a good idea, especially as we had plenty of horses around because my mother had been unable to resist buying them! We thought of Mandy, who was then twenty-two, knowing that she was talented and very hard-working. So an invitation was issued to her and it was promptly accepted.

Both Mandy and I have separate strings of horses. There was never any suggestion that she should bring on the novices for me to take over when they had gained experience. One or two horses may be switched around, because we feel they would be better suited to the other rider, and a couple are likely to be sold to help the Ivyleaze finances. But the main idea has always been that Mandy should eventually have the chance of riding at the major three-day events when she and the horses are ready for the big challenge.

Our new rider (like myself!) has a horsy mother, who taught her to ride almost as soon as she was out of her pram. She was still quite small when her second pony arrived amidst great excitement, in the family's brand-new trailer. He was a chestnut gelding of about 12.2 hands and

Mandy was impatient for him to be tacked up so that she could ride him. 'We went for a trot across a huge field,' she recalls, 'and, when we reached the top, the pony decided that he wanted to go back to the gateway. So he dropped his shoulder, deposited me on the ground and galloped back down the hill.

'My mother had caught him by the time I returned, sobbing and wiping my eyes, saying that I wouldn't ride the pony ever again. "You're totally useless and hopeless," said my mother. "It's obvious that I'll have to sort the pony out." So on she got and went trotting up the field, where the little pony proceeded to do exactly the same thing, this time leaving my mother in an embarrassed heap on the ground.'

They do say that horses are great levellers – and the same is obviously true of ponies! Mandy went on to ride working ponies as a child – two or three belonging to her family and some owned by other people. Later she rode in the Pony Club Horse Trials Championships, reaching the finals on four occasions. She also competed in the 1982 Junior European Championships at Rotherfield Park, where she finished ninth on Free Agent.

Smiley Begorrah has a lesson in discipline from Dorothy

It cannot have been easy for Mandy to abandon her own ideas and adopt the Ivyleaze way of doing things, but she has done so very cheerfully. She says that she came to us with the intention of absorbing everything that was said and learning from it. She was probably better able than most to fit in with our methods, which involve planning everything down to the last tiny detail. 'I've always realized, even with the ponies, that you need to be very clued up and think of everything,' she says, 'though I certainly never did it to quite the same extent!'

Mandy had four of our horses to ride in the spring of 1987 – two dark-brown seven-year-olds, Freeway and Beneficial, and two five-year-olds, Smiley Begorrah and Private Rose. She says that they all have their own characters but, if forced to pick a favourite, it would have to be Beneficial. 'I love the way Ben starts squealing, bucking and kicking when you get him to a competition. I don't know of any other horse that says "Let me get at it" in quite the same way.'

Ben almost missed his chance of 'getting at it' in April 1987, at Tidworth, where he had been entered for his first intermediate and Freeway was due to run in the Open Intermediate. My mother wanted to withdraw them both after Mandy had an accident in the lorry that morning, badly scalding her leg when a pot of boiling water tipped over. It was stinging badly and had begun to blister, making her own breeches too tight for taking a walk to see the Tidworth medical officer.

'There's only thing for it,' said Dot, 'you'll have to borrow my trousers.'

The two of them are built somewhat differently! Mandy must have looked quite a sight as she hitched Dot's trousers up and trundled off to get treatment for her injured leg. As luck would have it, Jane Starkey then went in search of Dot among the horseboxes and was shocked to the core at finding her trouserless. Her eyes were out on stalks when she asked whether Dorothy would be kind enough to stand in for one of the dressage judges who had failed to turn up.

'Poor Heather was running back and forth,' says Mandy, remembering my mother's hurried trips between the medical room and the lorry, where the newly recruited dressage judge was now urgently awaiting the return of her trousers. Fortunately, they arrived in the nick of time!

Mandy's leg was now bandaged and she said that it was no longer hurting. She wanted to ride both horses, but agreed she would see how it felt while walking the cross-country course, leaving my mother to work Beneficial in for the dressage. No one watching that day would have dreamt Mandy had anything wrong with her. She had a wonderful ride on Ben to finish on the same score as Mary Thomson, who won on King Max. Mandy took second place, having been slightly slower across country, and she also jumped clear on Freeway.

My mother bought Freeway in Devon from John Chapel who had sold Night Cap to us. Beneficial came to us as a yearling; his chief recommendation at the time was that (like Priceless and Night Cap) he is a son of Ben Faerie. We have had plenty of time to study his mischievous character, including those traits which are not always appreciated by any poor horse that has to share a field with him. He is a busy-body and a pest, forever trying to goad his companion into going somewhere or doing something by nibbling his tail or rump.

On one occasion he drove Master Craftsman to the point of such exasperation that there was sudden and unexpected retaliation. Crafty went at him with his ears flat back and literally chased him around the field until he had him cornered; Ben's only means of escape was to jump out, over a large hedge with a big drop down to the road. It was a dangerous leap, but luckily Ben was unharmed.

Nowadays Crafty goes out in the field with Freeway, who is too much of a scaredy cat to give him any hassle. One of the younger horses has to put up with Ben's pestering. They are all far more tolerant than Crafty, who regards such behaviour as beneath his dignity and therefore something to be nipped very firmly in the bud.

My mother, who regards Master Craftsman as the best of my horses, sees Smiley Begorrah as the potential star of Mandy's string. She bought him on a day trip to Ireland in August 1986, a few months before we found Ballyhack in Co. Wexford. Dot went with her on the day trip, but she was not a particularly alert companion. Having taken a few too many pills to avoid feeling sick on the journey, it was more than Dorothy could do to stay awake! Smiley was quick to take my mother's fancy. 'I liked him when I saw him playing around loose in the school in Ireland,' she says. 'He was obviously quite a character and he gave me the impression that he wasn't frightened of anything.'

Though described as chestnut, Smiley has extraordinary colouring – with a lot of black splodges and many white hairs that make him almost roan on one side. We have been left in no doubt since he arrived at Ivyleaze that he is indeed quite a character. We often see him with his head twisted round to the right over his stable door so that he can watch everything that goes on in the arena, which is only just visible from his box.

His most remarkable feat is performed when we put him out in the mud patch that we use during the winter. The grass on the other side of the fence looks to be way out of reach, until Smiley puts his head between the railings and elongates his neck to an amazing length. When he has eaten the grass on that patch, he gets down on his knees and does the giraffe act with his neck again to reach another grassy area.

Mandy recognizes his enormous talent and thinks it will take some time to tap; 'Smiley's not easy because he has such a quick brain; it will take a lot of patience to get him listening to me.'

We bought Private Rose, the fourth horse in Mandy's team, from Jane Starkey. He is a thoroughbred half brother of Bengal Lancer, the horse Jane is eventing herself, and he happens to be dark brown which is my mother's favourite colour.

For the Spring events of 1987, we also had the chestnut Water Polo, who was ridden by Elaine Pickworth until he was sold to Angie Rutherford (whose husband, Mike, is part of Genesis, the group that my mother and Dot enjoyed so much in Australia). Angie, who hunts and events, had already bought two other horses from us and we were confident she would enjoy the sweet-natured Water Polo. Elaine accepted his departure

Freeway and Mandy enjoying their first Open Intermediate together at Tidworth

in June 1987 without any hint of resentment. She said she was looking forward to riding one of the four-year-olds – Welton Chit Chat or Ben Hovis, who is a full brother to Night Cap.

Elaine came to us as a working pupil at the beginning of 1984, when she was sixteen. We slightly threw her into the deep end by making her Night Cap's groom at Badminton a few months later, with Dot keeping a careful eye on her. She also looked after Priceless until he left us to go hunting, and he was her great favourite. 'I really miss his cheeky face,' she says.

My mother wanted Elaine to have as many different rides as possible, so that she would be constantly learning about young horses. This arrangement suited her very well. 'I love riding the youngsters,' she says. 'It's so very satisfying and rewarding when they improve and mature, both in their way of going and their outlook on life.'

Welton Chit Chat had only just been backed when my mother and Dot went off on their Australian holiday, and it was Elaine who was given the responsibility of schooling him in their absence. 'That's when I had to put into practice all that I'd learnt here,' she recalls, a little anxiously. 'There were no major problems, but my heart was rather in my mouth

Dorothy may be talented with horses, but there was a small problem when she washed her own pyjamas

when they came back from Australia to see how he was going. Fortunately, they were both pleased with him.'

I was at home to help Elaine during their absence and one day, as I watched her jumping Water Polo, I realized that they weren't quite getting it together. There was nothing desperately wrong but, for some unknown reason, she seemed to have lost her ability to see a stride. I knew she could do so much better and it suddenly clicked that it must be her mental outlook that was wrong.

Mandy in Dot's trousers

'What are you thinking about when you're cantering round?' I asked.

'I'm thinking about the horse.'

'Well stop concentrating on the horse and think about your own position and how you're going to see a stride into the fence.'

It was interesting because we actually cracked it. She had been concentrating so hard on keeping the horse balanced and rounded that she was forgetting the main object of the exercise, which was to see a stride to that particular fence. When she forgot about the horse, we found that she was still getting him to move correctly, though it was now done subconsciously.

Elaine has patches, which I have experienced often enough myself, when her confidence is at a low ebb. I have a poem, given to me by Mike and Judy Tandy who are fence judges at Weston Park Horse Trials, which is a marvellous help in times of self-doubt. I gave a copy to Elaine and she has also felt the benefit of these words:

> If you think you are beaten, you are
> If you think you dare not, you don't
> If you'd like to win, but think you can't
> It's almost certain you won't.
> If you think you'll lose, you've lost
> For out of the world we find
> Success begins with a fellow's will
> It's all in the state of mind.
> If you think you're outclassed, you are
> You've got to think high to rise
> You've got to be sure of yourself before
> You can ever win a prize.
> Life's battles don't always go
> To the stronger or faster man
> But sooner or later the man who wins
> Is the one who thinks he can.
>
> *Anonymous*

This may not sound too much in the spirit of Baron de Coubertin, founder of the modern Olympics, who said that it is not winning that is important, but taking part. I do, in fact, entirely agree with him. On the other hand, I want to do everything to the best of my ability and sometimes my moral, needs a bit of a boost before I can go out and do just that.

CHAPTER SEVEN

Retired Sergeant Major

In my view, Priceless is the most intelligent horse that has ever looked through a bridle. I may, of course, be prejudiced because this son of Ben Faerie has used his brain so often on my behalf that I am bound to think him exceptional. But there are others, besides myself, who also regard him as a bit of a genius.

Lady Hugh Russell used to tell me that there was no real need to study the cross-country course when I was due to ride Priceless; all I had to do was pin the map up in his stable. Louise Bates, who is joint-master of the Pytchley foxhounds and began hunting him at the beginning of 1987, is equally impressed by his brain power.

'He's always watching hounds, ready to anticipate which way they're going to run,' she says. 'There's never any need for me to tell him where to go or when to turn, he works all that out for himself just by watching. It's uncanny to ride a horse that's so intelligent; he seems almost human.'

Priceless was the second of the Ben Faerie sons bought by my mother. We already had Night Cap and were so pleased with him that my mother decided she would like another by the same sire. She therefore tracked down the stallion's owner, Diana Scott, who said that she had just one Ben Faerie horse, a five-year-old she was using as her own hunter. So off we went to see the bay gelding and bought him the same day.

He was already called Priceless, thanks to a chance remark by Diana's sister, who saw him as a small foal and said, 'What a priceless little thing.' Little did she know how appropriate the name would seem in later years.

My mother had one of her 'feelings' about the five-year-old hunter. 'I can't explain it,' she says. 'No one could ever have called Priceless handsome and yet there was something about him that appealed to me very much. I go by an instinctive feeling; the technical part is Dorothy's department. She picks them to pieces, looks at how they move, where they put their feet and so on.'

Fortunately, Dot was not around when we bought Priceless. She gave her own disparaging opinion when she first saw him; in her view this latest acquisition might make a decent riding club horse, but he would never go any further. My mother was poleaxed by these dismissive words; needless to say, she has never let poor Dot forget them.

It has to be said that Priceless had few ardent fans when he first started eventing – and all of them were closely connected with Ivyleaze. He seemed, to us at least, to be making wonderful progress in the sport when he won Bramham as a six-year-old and finished sixth at Burghley the following year. By now, I was fondly imagining that P was about to take me towards the top of the eventing ladder, but was promptly brought down to earth by being told that he couldn't gallop and would therefore never get inside the optimum time at a three-day event. This assessment was, I am delighted to say, proved totally false. Priceless is not a fast horse

The baby Priceless. As a five-year old there are clear similarities between P and Ballyhack

but he can gallop and jump in rhythm, which is far more important in three-day eventing. He has, in my opinion, disproved the widely held belief that you need a wonderful racehorse to get inside the time. I would still argue against this belief, even though I now have two speed merchants myself in Murphy and Master Craftsman.

Priceless took me to my first European Championship (at Horsens in Denmark in 1981) and to the World Championships the following year (at Luhmühlen in Germany). We won team gold medals on both occasions and I was looking forward to more championships when, during December 1982, he suddenly became desperately ill. We were at our wits' end as we watched him standing in his stable with his head lowered, rocking very slightly and getting thinner by the hour. We were waiting for the results of blood samples when I went off on my own to my sponsors' party and stopped off to buy Murphy Himself on the way. I sometimes wonder whether I would have gone to look at the big grey horse had I not been feeling so low and wanting something to take my mind off the invalid at home.

We would have lost P had it not been for Don Attenburrow, who diagnosed a bacterial infection called Leptospirosis, which is usually carried in mouse or rat excreta. Antibiotics and glucose were prescribed. We organized a twenty-four hour rota so that we could monitor his condition by day and night – and, thank God, at the end of six exhausting weeks the crisis was over. The bottom would have dropped out of my world had we lost this down-to-earth chap, with his small piggy eyes and amazing brain.

He had three-day events so well sussed out that he knew exactly what was coming and where to conserve his energy. He did roads and tracks at a sullen trot, often worrying me silly as I began to wonder whether he was fit enough for the cross-country. During the ten-minute halt he would stand like a zombie, looking more like a tired cab horse than an eventer who was about to face thirty-odd solid cross-country fences. He would then, quite literally, leap into life as soon as I prepared to get on him. He almost bowled over our precious chef d'équipe, Major Malcolm Wallace, when he was rearing and playing the fool before the start of the Olympic cross-country in Los Angeles.

Priceless had missed the spring events of 1983 because of his illness, but he was fighting fit by the autumn when he won Burghley and, again for the Olympics the following year, when he endangered Wol's life before winning a team silver and individual bronze medal. The heady joy of jumping a clear cross-country round for our team in Los Angeles – finishing within a second of the optimum time – left me feeling as high as if I'd drunk a magnum of champagne.

Then another crisis occurred. Welton Elan, whom we have since sold, kicked P while they were out in the field together at the end of September 1984. It seemed insignificant until a lump appeared on P's near fore; when she saw this worrying sign of damage, my mother quickly contacted Don Attenburrow, who discovered that there was a hairline fracture just above the knee. P had to be confined to his stable, except when he was led out very slowly four times a day and allowed to eat some grass. Once again we were all worried sick about him.

The Priceless brain was still ticking during his months of enforced inactivity. He was on a fairly strict diet, because we didn't want him to put on too much weight, and he strongly disapproved of having his rations reduced. He tried banging on his door whenever he saw Elaine, who was looking after him, but soon realized that she was not going to give in.

Then Priceless decided that my mother might be a soft touch. 'He used to watch everything that was going on outside his box,' says Elaine, 'and whenever he spotted Heather he immediately started banging his door. She was obviously worried about him straining his leg, so she quite often relented and gave him some hay. He was very quick to realize that she was his only chance.'

I was not totally preoccupied with concern about Priceless during those months he spent in his stable; I was also thinking about the new man in my life: Hamish Leng. I had met him at a lunch party given by our great friend, Moysie Barton, shortly after P's fracture was discovered. I thought this tall, dark stranger was very good-looking and was distinctly peeved when he scarcely seemed to notice my presence either before or during lunch. But an unexpected letter followed that first meeting and one date led to another, until we were seeing each other almost every day.

I joined Hamish in Kenya during December that year and, late on Christmas Eve, he asked me to marry him. This was also completely unexpected, but I had no need to linger over my answer. 'Of course I will,' I said. I was already dotty about the giant of 6 feet $4\frac{1}{2}$ inches, whose feet are so big that I reckon he could come flying down a snow-clad mountain without skis.

Priceless had been left in the care of my mother, Dot and Elaine. We were still hoping that he might go to Badminton in the spring of 1985 and, after returning to England with an engagement to announce, I had to find out whether it would be safe to run him at our big local event. As always, we turned to Don Attenburrow for guidance.

Don has the only practice in Europe that uses scintigraphy to investigate bone injuries. It involves injecting a special chemical with radio isotopes attached; these make straight for the bone, concentrating in those areas where healing is still taking place. With the help of this method, we were able to establish that the bone had mended. Priceless could therefore go to Badminton and, as though to celebrate being back on full rations, he won the Whitbread Trophy there for the first time. In the autumn, he enhanced his record still further by winning the European Championships at Burghley, jumping the big course almost nonchalantly to give me a magical ride, probably the best I'll ever have across country.

I had serious misgivings about taking P to the other side of the globe to compete at the World Championships in May 1986. Would the long journey to Australia take too much out of him? Did it amount to abusing this wonderful horse, who had already done so much for me? These questions gave me some troubled nights, both before and after the decision to compete at Gawler in South Australia was taken.

The fears subsided after I had flown halfway round the world to find Priceless looking remarkably fit and well after his own separate journey.

Priceless checking out the neighbours

Dot had accompanied him on the plane, giving much more thought to his well-being than her own comfort. Elaine flew out with my mother and took over as groom when she arrived. She had been with P at Wylye, where the horses were in quarantine for a month before the trip, and she is convinced he already knew something important was in prospect.

'He had a little clock working in his brain and he always knew what was coming up,' she says. 'He'd been to Wylye before for team concentrations, so he realized he must be there for something special.'

We had four weeks in Australia before the World Championships began and we had to be firm in resisting the all too obvious temptation to overdo the training. I think we were all glad when the week of the competition arrived. I had a special reason to be pleased, because it was at that stage Hamish flew out to join me, his arrival cleverly timed to coincide with various parties.

There are many indelible memories of the competition. They include P's bucks before we went into the dressage arena, when he knew he had me over a barrel and that all I could do was sit and pray. He let rip again at the end of the test, with some more bucks and about four flying changes but, fortunately, the rest of his work was good and we were sixth at the end of the dressage.

Left: Priceless on course for his world title

Below: Not a pas de deux! Mark Todd and Charisma have finished their dressage at Gawler; Priceless and I are about to start ours

There were twenty-six falls from forty-three starters on the next day's cross-country, but my incredible horse once again carried me safely round and we moved up to second place, some 17 points behind New Zealand's Judith 'Tinks' Pottinger on Volunteer. The Kiwis were also leading for the team title until the entire situation was changed the following morning, when Volunteer failed the veterinary inspection. I was looking through some photographs when I heard this devastating news and I promptly went in search of poor Tinks. We fell into each other's arms, both in floods of tears; anyone watching would have found it hard to tell whether I was giving or receiving consolation.

I was now in the lead for the world title and the butterflies were working overtime as I waited for the show jumping, wrestling with the familiar fear of ruining everything by taking the wrong course or starting before the bell. I managed to avoid either of these errors and Priceless, as always aware of the importance of the occasion, jumped out of his skin over the big course for a clear round. New Zealand's Trudy Boyce, who had been a popular member of the Ivyleaze team when she spent six months with us as a working pupil, was silver medallist, retrieving something for the wonderfully sporting Kiwis.

'Didn't we have some party afterwards!' Tinks said, when she came to England the following year. 'That was the best part of the whole trip; it was so good it even made Australian television.'

The Brits can confirm that it certainly was some party. Our winning team – Clissy Strachan, Ian Stark, Lorna Clarke (who was individual bronze medallist) and myself – were deafened by the din from the Kiwi tent as we held our own lively celebrations, so we went in to join the New Zealand rave-up. At one stage I climbed onto a table with the German rider, Claus Erhorn, and we both stood there singing and swaying until the inevitable happened and the table collapsed. About four weeks later, while I was lifting some furniture, my neck became completely locked and it stayed that way for several days. I was told that I must have had a severe fall within the last month; I knew exactly where and how this had happened, but I felt it was prudent to keep the details to myself!

The Kiwis and Aussies invited us to another party the following night in Gawler, where we played a daft game which was similar to Cardinal Bluff. If you gave the wrong answer, you had to drink a glass of wine, which became rather drastic in my case because I was wrong eight times in a row. Not wishing to let down the Poms, I abided by the rules and felt distinctly groggy as I fell into bed at 2.30 a.m. knowing that I would have to be up again about an hour later for the start of the journey home.

'I'm never going to touch another drop,' I said to my team-mates and fellow travellers. But this resolution was short-lived. Once on the aeroplane, we were all offered a glass of champagne and I promptly persuaded myself that it would be churlish to turn it down.

Both Tinks and Trudy came to England with the intention of competing in the 1987 Whitbread Championships at Badminton and, considering the distance they had travelled, the event's cancellation must have been a bigger blow to them than anyone else. We had a fair-sized Kiwi contingent at the lunch party my mother gave on the Sunday, which would have been the show-jumping day. It included Tinks and Trudy, Mark and Caroline Todd, with whom they were based in Wiltshire, Tinks's husband, Andy, and the team vet, Wally Niederer.

By then Priceless had retired to the hunting field. He had added the British National title to his World and European championships a few months after Gawler, when he finished second at Gatcombe to J. J. Babu, ridden by Bruce Davidson of the United States. I had dithered about making the decision to retire him, at first thinking that I would leave it to him; he would be bound to let me know when he wanted to call it a day. But the idea of giving him a new life as a hunter took shape and began to seem right. He had always loved the cross-country phase of a

Champagne celebrations at Gawler. Priceless's breeder, Diana Scott, with my mother, myself and Dot

three-day event and was not over-enthusiastic about his dressage, which was beginning to deteriorate; hunting would be a way of rewarding him for all he had done for us.

I rode him myself with the Duke of Beaufort's pack before he went to Louise and, because I was concerned that he might misbehave, I didn't

Left: *I am the greatest!*

Right: *The Pytchley's joint-master, Louise Bates, and the world three-day event champion, Priceless, team up to enjoy their mutual love of hunting*

clip him beforehand. He looked fairly woolly and not at all like a world champion when we arrived at the meet, where various people asked me what I was riding.

'Just one of the horses in the yard,' I told them.

When asked again at the end of the day, after Priceless had given me the most marvellous ride and behaved impeccably, I was rather more forthcoming.

'It's Priceless,' I said with a grin.

I hunted him seven times with the Beaufort, usually following Lord Patrick Beresford, who had taken over from Malcolm Wallace as chef d'équipe of the British three-day event team in 1985. Patrick has a brilliant hunter, a former polo pony called Buck, and I knew I would have an exciting time if I kept close behind him. Also I knew that I wouldn't get myself into trouble by being in the wrong place at the wrong time. If Patrick happens to make a mistake like that, I thought, I can always blame it on him because he's leading me! He can't have been too fed up at having me tagging along behind, since he commissioned a lovely painting of Buck and Priceless out hunting together.

I delivered Priceless to Louise in Northamptonshire the day before Hamish and I went away on holiday. It had been a difficult decision to let him leave Ivyleaze, albeit temporarily, because he is such a great friend and we all love him dearly. On the other hand, it seemed unfair to keep him at home doing nothing when he still loves to be out jumping fences. I only have a chance to hunt him during November and December, so he will come back to us for those two months each year – and he can be assured of a huge welcome!

He will also be warmly welcomed when he returns to Louise for the remainder of the season. She now raves about him. 'His manners are super and he gives me such confidence; he always sees his own stride and the bigger the fence the better he jumps; I've never had a hunter like him.'

For his part, the retired Sergeant Major is equally happy to be carrying the Pytchley's joint-master. Louise says that he automatically moves into a higher gear as soon as he hears the huntsman's horn.

CHAPTER EIGHT

Grand Old Man

Dubonnet, who celebrated his twenty-first birthday in 1987, has to have a very special place in my heart. He was the game little horse who gave me my first taste of eventing and had to put up with a seemingly endless succession of mistakes from his clueless rider.

We first met when I was eleven and he was a little colt of six months, who had just been parted from his mother and sent off to be sold at Five Lanes Cattle Market. He was bought there for £35 by Ewart Rice, my grandfather, who promptly delivered him to us. My mother was not best pleased. She was used to her father turning up with lorry loads of ponies, and was frequently exasperated with him, but this arrival was particularly badly timed. We happened to be in the final stages of preparing to go and live in the Philippines, where my father had been posted as Military Attaché, and there were quite enough complications without having to worry about this little foal.

'What on earth did you want to buy that for?' asked my mother.

My grandfather thought she was being totally unreasonable. He had never appreciated the enormous amount of work involved in breaking and schooling all the ponies he had delivered to her. 'We'll see,' he said, in his haughtiest manner. 'Anyway, the colt's for Virginia.'

I didn't give a toss whether the colt made 15.2 or not. I was eleven years old and bursting with pride at the thought that I now owned my first horse. I left them to argue it out.

My grandfather's addiction for buying horses and ponies (which my mother has inherited) had already brought a great deal of fun into my

life, though it has to be said that I was not much help in looking after
them. One evening I had been sent out to count them – I think we had
sixteen ponies at the time – and I am afraid that I performed my task in
a shamefully slapdash way.

'They're all fine,' I said, when I came back indoors, leaving the ponies
to their night in the orchard.

It was only when my mother went out to make her own count
the following morning that we realized one of them was missing. We
eventually found the poor pony stuck between two trees, with a telltale
pile of droppings behind to show that he must have been there since the
previous day. He was so firmly wedged that one tree had to be cut down
in order to release him.

Dubonnet (or Dubby as we usually call him) was left in the capable
hands of a great friend, Rosemary Thomas, while we were away in the
Philippines. I then became a boarder at Bedgebury Park in Kent and rarely
saw my chestnut horse until I left school at the age of sixteen. By then he
had grown from a gangly colt into a sturdy five-year-old of 15.3 hands –
which, as my grandfather was pleased to point out at every available
opportunity, was one inch higher than my mother's predicted limit. We
were then living in Devon and, having been released from boarding
school, I was looking forward with rising excitement to riding Dubby in
local competitions.

Our first contest was a show-jumping class at a local gymkhana, where
we were eliminated for three refusals. I'm ashamed to say that I burst into
tears as I rode out of the ring. My mother was on hand to put me right
on this score (as on so many others) by telling me that I must learn to be
a good sportswoman. No matter how disappointed I might be, I was not
to dissolve into tears again. We have all indulged in them on other
occasions, such as when Priceless won Badminton, but I have learnt to
grin and bear when disappointment strikes!

In those early days, I was lucky enough to be living near the Strachan
sisters, Sally and Clissy. Sally nobly took me on for lessons, putting me
through hours of dreaded flat work until I was totally exhausted. Looking
back, I realize that I owe her a huge debt for giving me this grounding,
even though I may have failed to appreciate it at the time.

There were still plenty of occasions that had to be met with the grin-
and-bear it routine. I was eliminated on three more all too memorable
days at the early one-day events with Dubby, each time for a different
reason. First it was for three refusals at a cross-country fence. Then, to my
much greater mortification, I started before the show-jumping bell when
I was a member of the Silverton Pony Club team that would otherwise
have qualified for the final of the Horse Trials Championships. In my first

British Horse Society one-day event, I managed to miss out two cross-country fences, without realizing it until the letter E was chalked on the scoreboard. All this may have been character-building, but I could have done without it!

There were also days to be remembered for quite different reasons. Dubonnet was with us long before we acquired our smart Citibank Savings lorry; we used to travel to events in an ancient Land-Rover with the horse behind in a trailer. On one of these journeys I recall having to make a stupid confession after we had gone about five miles.

'I'm terribly sorry,' I said to my mother, 'but I'm afraid I've forgotten my hat.'

She responded with all the usual things that mothers say on these occasions. 'How could you be so stupid? Do I have to run around after you the whole time to make sure that you don't forget something so important? I can't imagine how you expect me to do a U-turn with a

Cirencester, 1973. For such a small chap, Dubonnet had an enormous jump

trailer on the back.'

She then looked behind her and gaped. There was no trailer on the back – I had forgotten my hat and she had forgotten the horse! We laughed until the tears ran down our cheeks on the way back home, where we found a slightly bewildered Dubonnet waiting patiently in the abandoned trailer.

Dubby and I progressed slowly as we learnt together and eventually we did our first three-day event at Tidworth, where I was competing in the selection trial for the Junior European Championships. Walking the

I must have been told to keep my head up during the dressage phase of the Junior European Championships

course there with Clissy Strachan was one of the most alarming experiences of my life. My mother, who had set out with us, was so appalled when she saw the fourth fence – a vast, deep ditch with a stream running through it – that she turned back. 'That's it,' she said, 'I'm not going any further.'

Because I was generating so much electricity that day, my watch stopped whenever I put it on my wrist. As on many other occasions, Uncle Jack came to the rescue by buying me a brand new stop-watch, which has never let me down. Now I also have one of the Ebel watches that are made especially for sports-people; it has also coped efficiently with the electrical charge I give it when the adrenalin is flowing and it has always kept ticking.

Having walked the Tidworth course with my heart in my mouth, Dubby gave me a wonderful clear round over it. I must have bored everyone to tears for months afterwards as I described all the thrilling leaps and the near misses over and over again. Another dream came true when we were chosen for an individual place in the 1972 Junior European Championships to be held at Eridge, where the final trial for the Olympic team was also taking place.

I was completely in awe of all the great riders at Eridge, where Dubby and I had a fall at the third cross-country fence from home. This almost became a source of pride when I saw the names of the others who fell there. Mark Phillips and Richard Meade, plus the United States riders James Wofford and Michael Plumb, were victims of the same fence – a

Girls will be girls! Galloping flat out after the prize-giving at the Junior European Championships

rail over a ditch, landing onto a bank that had become as slippery as a ski-run after torrential rain.

My greatest moment with Dubby came the following year when we won the individual Junior European title at Pompadour in France and were also members of the winning British team. My grandfather was just as chuffed as I was; this was another heaven-sent opportunity to remind my mother of her words when she first saw the colt he had bought for me at Five Lanes Cattle Market.

Though he completed Badminton in 1974, Dubby was not really up to the minimum weight of 11 stone 11 pounds in senior three-day events and we retired him a year or so later. I have since used him for many lecture/demonstrations and he still earns his keep as schoolmaster to the working pupils (while they learn to do half-pass, shoulder-in and so on), but he gave up jumping in 1985 when he was beginning to feel a little stiff.

I normally find any horse boring until I can get on it and leap over fences; the babies don't interest me until they are old enough to jump. My mother and Dot love working with them before they reach this stage – and I am more than happy to let them get on with it.

But Dubonnet is different. Looking at his intelligent chestnut head with its white blaze brings back many cherished memories. He is the only horse in our yard that can claim to be a founder member of the Ivyleaze team.

Dubonnet at the age of twenty-one